WRITING FICTION FOR CHILDREN

Writing Fiction for Children

Stories Only You Can Tell

JUDY K. MORRIS

University of Illinois Press
Urbana and Chicago

© 2001 by Judy K. Morris

All rights reserved

Manufactured in the United States of America

C 5 4 3 2 1

♾ This book is printed on acid-free paper.

Library of Congress Cataloging-in-Publication Data

Morris, Judy K.

Writing fiction for children : stories only you can tell / Judy K. Morris.

p.   cm.

ISBN 0-252-02686-1

1. Children's literature—Authorship.

I. Title.

PN147.5.M67   2001

808.06'83—dc21   00-013103

For Hugh Morris
and
Willa Day Morris

Once upon a time . . . and, happily, ever after.

Contents

Acknowledgments

Many people contributed to the making of this book. My thanks to them all.

Members of my workshops helped me with their hard questions, their laughter, and their intense commitment to writing books for children.

I'm deeply grateful to Al Lefcowitz and Jane Fox, as are many writers in the greater Washington, D.C., area, for the Writer's Center, a place for writers to teach and learn.

Those who read the book in draft, early and late—Jonas Morris, Bill Reiss, Sarah Toth, Hugh Morris, Kate Kazan, Jeff Prince, Dale Appleman, Rebecca Todd, Nick Kazan, Willa Day Morris—were encouraging, honest, and helpful: true gifts. Lisa Kiely made a crucial professional contribution.

Jacqueline Woodson, Kathleen Karr, Jane Conly, and other writers took the time to tell me how they go about writing children's novels, which was most helpful.

The people at the University of Illinois Press, Ann Lowry in particular, have been wonderfully thoughtful, constructive, and open-minded. Betsy Hearne and Deborah Stevenson, who vetted the manuscript for the Press, gave conceptual and editorial help for which I'm very grateful.

Particularly happy thanks are due Ann Tobias, children's book editor (though not of my books) and serendipitous, kind friend. Ann suggested that I try teaching a workshop and later that I write this book. Her thoughts and perceptions, absorbed and confronted in hours and years of conversation, and above all her unwavering conviction that books for children should be wonderful, are echoed in every chapter.

Without whom, indeed.

WRITING FICTION FOR CHILDREN

Introduction
A Guide to the Toolbox

Can Writing Be Taught?

> So, with Spartan firmness, the young authoress laid her first-
> born on her table, and chopped it up as ruthlessly as any ogre.
> In the hope of pleasing every one, she took every one's advice;
> and, like the old man and his donkey in the fable, suited
> nobody.
>
> —Louisa May Alcott, *Little Women*

Can writing be taught? In one sense, everyone already knows how to tell a story: we tell small stories to each other every day.

More important, the wellspring of a good story rises from deep inside. The power of and pleasure from a well-written book grow in large part from the author's strong feeling for the story and the individual voice that tells it. Can someone on the outside truly help?

There *are* ways to help people write the story they want to write. My own sense of this developed slowly, from many parts of my life: growing up in a home where the work and pleasures of reading and writing were taken seriously; working with stimulating teachers; living with my own children; reading adults' and children's novels; writing novels for children; teaching children to write; teaching adults who are writing for children.

For almost twenty years I taught one or two writing classes a week in the Washington, D.C., elementary schools. I began to teach for many reasons. The most important was purely selfish: teaching would keep me close to children as I did my own writing.

At first I didn't know just what I had to offer. Often I arrived at a school at recess. The yard was full of action; the air was full of words: shouts, whispers, taunts, cheers . . . and stories, I was sure. Twenty minutes later, the same children, now sweaty and exhausted, their faces streaked from perfunctory washing, sat at their desks with papers entirely blank. They couldn't think of a thing to write about, they told me. They couldn't think of a word. I learned how wide the gap can feel between knowing a story, telling it to someone, and writing it down.

Soon I discovered ways to help fourth, fifth, and sixth graders find what they could say on paper. My doubts began to fade. Most useful were an absolute conviction that each child had stories to tell and the realization that in a writing class there was no need for everyone to write the same way, to work at the same level. Writing isn't like math, I told the children; there's no one (right) answer. There's only you and what and how you choose to write. There are stories, real and imaginary, that only you in all the world can tell.

The children certainly did have stories to tell, often surprising ones. At the end of one year a good little girl who had written only sweet and boring adult-pleasing pieces turned in a long, complex story about a boy who got into trouble for sassing his mean teacher. The boy disappeared for several days, then returned to school with a life-size puppet he could control. Before long the smart-aleck puppet "got up and smacked the teacher." Once the girl's story had placed her at a safe remove from the action . . . pow!

One fourth grader turned in a single sentence, crudely lettered yet brilliantly imagined, for an assignment meant to call forth a page—and a half hour—of work. I read it, then reread it. She'd done everything I had asked—in one sentence! (This girl also had confounded school authorities. She was about to be put into a class for learning disabled children when her grandmother protested; she was put into a talented and gifted section instead.) As her classmates worked on, I excused her to go off into the rewarding realm of her own mind.

Such students were teaching me: with a person or a manuscript, wait, watch, learn. Leave space and time for the mysteries to evolve.

After I'd been teaching children for ten years, a friend asked me to start a workshop with her for adults who wanted to write for children. Again unsure, I began by using lessons from my school classes; sometimes the exercises from my daytime classroom were repeated in my dining room table workshop that evening. Many exercises can be helpful to people at any age, at any skill level.

Of course, there were differences between the child and adult students. When writing summaries of their plots, children never seemed to get to the end but bogged down in the middle, where the action was. Adults tended to leave out the middle in their rush to the end, where the lesson was. Kids had to be encouraged to find the stories they could tell by getting them to talk out loud about their ideas and memories. Adults often had to be kept from talking, from dissipating their stories into the air rather than confronting the real challenge: how to tell their stories on paper.

Another problem soon developed. The adults began writing to engage and amuse each other. This was pleasant, but the point was how *children*—their readers—would react. As a writer and a teacher, I've learned to keep children present in every way possible. In Rudyard Kipling's *Just So Stories*, which he first told to his own children, he often addresses his listener-readers with the interjection, "O Best Beloved." I think of this as a reminder that writing for children is the loving telling of stories to those who are just beginning—who are struggling!—to understand the world as it is and as it might be.

Listening to hundreds of smart, engaged workshop members talk about manuscripts and books has taught me more. They've made plots hum that I wouldn't have dared to attempt. People brought in well-loved novels that I'd never heard of. Enthusiastic comments about a manuscript that I'd thought was so-so made me look again to find out why it seemed to work after all. Often I'd hear someone—even myself—say something useful; I'd jot a hasty note and go home to revise a chapter.

Little by little, as I wrote and published more books and continued to teach in schools, as the reading group I belonged to showed me over and over how differently individuals respond to the same story, as my workshop (I was now teaching alone) moved to a writing center full of able writer-teachers, I became confident that I had something to offer beginning writers about how stories work, how writers write, how children read.

Adults writing for children, I found, have some common problems:

- plotting awkwardly, with no clear sense of the story's framework, instead of seizing what is crucial and dynamic;
- overloading the beginning of a story with exposition;
- knowing their intriguing beginning and rousing end but dismissing the entire midportion—the hero's struggle!—with something like, "after many adventures he comes to . . .";
- writing a thin story in order to avoid complexity; or the opposite: throwing in all kinds of scenes for immediate effect that, however charming, don't belong and weaken the story;
- in fantasies, announcing the rules at whim rather than building them into the characters and the setting;

- using a self-conscious, cute, preachy, or ponderous voice that annoys readers and takes attention away from the story;
- failing to convey on the page their energy and excitement about their story.

I had some answers for these problems. Certainly, the spark of the story, the impetus, the theme, and the flow of words must come from the writer's passion—no one else has much to do with that. But though what an author builds is up to her or him, there are tools every writer should know how to use. This book is a guide to the toolbox.

Reading, writing, teaching, and living have helped me develop a few basic beliefs about fiction written for children:

- Children's books should be hopeful. This doesn't mean that there are always happy endings but that the central characters are active on their own or others' behalf and that their actions have consequence and value. It's no coincidence that this framework makes for a good story.
- The writing, whether simple or complex, should be clear and consistent. Great care must be taken in communicating with the reader.
- It's natural for adults with strong beliefs and a treasure of information and experience to want to pass these on to children, but a book reeking of didacticism will soon be closed.
- Above all, children's stories should be thrilling, funny, interesting, touching . . . definitely a pleasure to read.

The child reader's satisfaction in a story comes from many elements: a provocative beginning; an interesting setting; an active, empathetic main character; pleasurable incidents; interesting words; a lively plot with unexpected—but no false—turns; a carefully prepared climax; a sense that the resolution is as it should be; a consistent, trustworthy voice; smoothness in the narrative progress; an absence of preaching; and beneath it all something at stake that matters.

Sometimes a mystique develops about the act of writing. But when you find some "wise" advice, it's quite possible you'll soon read or hear the opposite—and it will seem equally "wise." Some writers enjoy raging about rejection letters from editors who make conflicting comments about the same manuscript. But why should those editors agree about a story? Readers won't. So from my "wise" words that follow in this book I hope you'll take only what works for you, what meets your own needs.

For instance, should you plan and prepare intensively or should you let your story just flow from your mind? I suggest thorough planning, particularly of plot, because it works for me and because I've seen it help many people. However, some highly successful writers prefer less planning (see chapter 6). Perfectly good, perfectly wonderful, practically perfect stories and novels have been written this way.

In truth, there wouldn't be much to a book like this if all there was to say was, "Ruminate on your characters and their situation for a while, then sit down and write." Or, "Try becoming a conduit for a story and see what happens." This book, willy-nilly, must deal with concrete, practical methods. Even for nonplanners, these discussions may stimulate useful thoughts.

Embarking on writing a novel or a short story can be daunting. Don't be discouraged by all that's suggested here, because there's a lot to absorb. You might want to adopt a workshop approach, breaking the book into manageable bits—say, each week studying one chapter and doing the attendant exercises. You can use the exercises as you prepare to write or anywhere along the way, right down to your final revisions. (For a sense of how my suggestions might fit into an overall writing process, see chapter 22.)

A warning: Reading about writing is not writing. Although you may read this book through and work on every exercise, the time will come when you'll be back alone, wrestling with your story.

Here's a picture to keep in mind: a child, comfy in a chair, curled around your book and sinking into your story. Swimming smoothly or diving eagerly through it, this reader is oblivious even to the call to supper, reading deeply, totally absorbed. If you can keep that child immersed, moving through your story without breaking the surface of intense, committed belief, then finally, reluctantly, coming to the family table, your reader will hold within the thrilling sense of partaking in a secret life, unknown to anyone else.

Your reader inside your story, your story inside your reader. You couldn't hope for anything more wonderful.

Exercises and Inspiration

> For some reason, he began to think of the first things he could remember. Till a bat is two weeks old he's never alone: the little naked thing—he hasn't even any fur—clings to his mother wherever she goes. After that she leaves him at night; he and the other babies hang there sleeping, till at last their mothers come home to them. Sleepily, almost dreaming, the bat began to make up a poem about a mother and her baby.
> It was easier than the other poems, somehow.
>
> —Randall Jarrell, *The Bat-Poet*

Although this book may interest parents, teachers, librarians, and others who care about children's fiction, it's addressed particularly to people who have a story to tell.

A beginning writer once gave me some excellent advice about teaching: the most helpful exercises relate to the stories on which writers are working. So this book is written to be read actively, with every point connected to the story you're working on. Each chapter discusses an aspect of fiction writing, often using published novels for illustration, illumination, and analysis. At the ends of subsections and chapters are exercises that point you back into your own story and help to sharpen your skills for telling it.

A writer's work is a complex interplay between inspiration and practical application, between the intuitive, imaginative, expressive, creative mind and the controlling, ordering, editorial mind. Writing teachers speak primarily to this second mind, talking mostly about the how-to of writing.

Those of you who were hoping for inspiration here, as well as those who write without much preparation and don't want to be aware of the mechanics of your story building, may find these exercises helpful in feeding and stimulating your imagination. An exercise on listing the smells in a particular setting may lead to . . . anything. Use these exercises however they best serve you, either as you set out or when you're revising your story.

Having learned the importance of making exercises relevant to working stories, I have little use for "fishing" exercises aimed at dredging the subconscious to see what can be pulled up and used. If your story is rooted in your own feelings—a character you're curious about, an incident that tickles you, an image you're stuck on, a memory you treasure or fear—there's *plenty* going on in your subconscious to support and sustain the story. If you want to write it, trust yourself and start. Notice what's on your mind, muse on it, tumble it about, wallow in it. Write about what you care about.

If you'd like to write for children someday but don't yet have a story in mind, before you read further you might want to settle on a story to think about. You'll get more from advice on characters, say, if you have a specific character in mind. (The exercise at the end of this section may help.)

As you work on the exercises, indulge the wanderings of your mind. Let your imagination play freely over whatever suggests itself. Don't be too earnest at first. It doesn't really matter if you don't finish that list of smells today. If you actively make use of the exercises in this book, you should, in the end, have not only more tools to work with but also a sharper, deeper, richer sense of the story you're writing.

Although the exercises will help you analyze, understand, enrich, and shape your story, don't let them control your work once you actually begin to write. Step back from analysis then and welcome haphazard thoughts. Write freely, enjoying the flow of the action, your characters, the fun of discovery, and trust—for the moment—what feels right. My own way is to plan with care, then put the outlines, maps, lists, and character sketches aside and simply write my story. Later I go back and use the mechanics of writing to improve my work.

Children's stories are often read aloud, so reading aloud should be part of your writing process. You might read some of your finished exercises aloud to yourself or to someone else. You'll sense the quality of what you've written and possibly find the best voice with which to tell your story.

The exercises in this book may seem simple. They're not. They're basic and difficult. They're spare so that the creativity in doing them will be yours. Responding to them productively will take concentration and time. Many can usefully be done several times as you work on your story.

Exercise

The quote from *The Bat-Poet* at the beginning of this section shows inspiration at work. Instead of "For some reason, he began to think of the first things he could remember," try setting out to think about child-hood.

Make a list of the things in your childhood room or your children's rooms. Don't forget the intangibles, such as a curious shadow or eerie street sounds. If an item evokes a memory or story, forget the list and write down everything pertaining to that. There are reasons we remember, reasons an object evokes strong feeling: the swing hanging in the doorway, the pillow's softness have meaning for us. Perhaps you can mine some such memory for a story worth telling.

Reading as You Write

> Everybody said it was a real beautiful oath, and asked Tom if
> he got it out of his own head. He said, some of it, but the rest
> was out of pirate books and robber books.
>
> —Mark Twain, *The Adventures of Huckleberry Finn*

Reading and writing are parts of the same process. The act of writing is in part your careful reading of your own work. The act of reading fiction is in part the reader imaginatively, creatively making the story his or her own.

Reading and rereading published novels are attendant work for a writer—you must read widely and well to develop your sense of what fiction for children can be. Reading thoughtfully will also prepare you to understand an editor's comments.

Although most of this book is relevant to fiction for younger children and to young adult novels, it focuses on novels for people aged eight to twelve. This is a great, brief period in human lives when, newly able and confident, we look outward toward the greater world, developing a sense of our place and our possibilities. When, during the tumult of adolescence, we seek shelter back inside ourselves and a narrower world of peers, young adult novels seem to follow with plots more closely focused on individual growth and coming-of-age themes.

It's for the "middle-aged" children that most novels thought of as children's classics or near classics have been written, many more than can be discussed here. These include: *The Wind in the Willows* by Kenneth Grahame, *A Wrinkle in Time* by Madeleine L'Engle, *My Father's Dragon* by Ruth S. Gannett, *Mary Poppins* by P. L. Travers, *Peter Pan* by J. M. Barrie, *The Yearling* by Marjorie Kinnan Rawlings, *Beauty* by Robin McKinley, *The Borrowers* by Mary Norton, *The Sword in the Stone* by T. H. White, *The Lion, the Witch, and the Wardrobe* by C. S. Lewis, *The Phantom Tollbooth* by Norton Juster, *Mrs. Frisby and the Rats of NIMH* by Robert C. O'Brien, *Half Magic* by Edward Eager, *The Book of Three* by Lloyd Alexander, *The Wolves of Willoughby Chase* by Joan Aiken, *The Incredible Journey* by Sheila Burnford, and the Tripods trilogy by John Christopher.

Since no one knows which of the newer books will endure in children's hearts, the stories and novels used here to illustrate how setting, dialogue, and point of view work are mostly classics and likely to be familiar to most adult readers. Among them are "The Elephant's Child" by Rudyard Kipling, *Treasure Island* by Robert Louis Stevenson, *Charlotte's Web* by E. B. White, *The Adventures of Tom Sawyer* and *The Adventures of Huckleberry Finn* by Mark Twain, *Tuck Everlasting* by Natalie Babbitt, and the Ramona stories by Beverly Cleary.

Particular attention will be paid to three novels. *The Wonderful Wizard of Oz* by L. Frank Baum is a straightforward story, an American fantasy that illustrates many aspects of good writing for children. *Stone Fox* by John Reynolds Gardiner is a tale I love. It snuck up on me: finding it by chance, I was drawn in, then excited, then deeply moved. The sometimes-awkward writing is overcome by the strong, spare story of a child hero struggling toward an important goal. *Roll of Thunder, Hear My Cry* by Mildred D. Taylor is at once the personal story of a black family struggling to hold onto its 400 acres in the segregated South of the 1930s and a huge Victorian novel for children, rich in settings and in child and adult characters from family, school, and several larger communities.

If you read these or other children's novels along with this book, staying alert to your needs and pleasures as a reader, you can test my comments and suggestions, test the authors whose work you're reading. If you're unfamiliar with children's novels, you might begin a planned reading program. If you've read children's books since you were six, don't stop now. You're working to become part of a tradition.

Read—and reread—good novels, mediocre novels, and your old favorites. Read the classics and the books from ten or twenty years ago that seem on their way to becoming classics. Read also contemporary novels published for the age group you're writing for to get a feel for these stories.

When you find a novel you think is wonderful, recommend it to others, children and adults. We need to help each other ferret out the best from the more than five thousand children's books published each year. In addition to the recent children's novels discussed later, others I've enjoyed are *The Thief* by Megan Whalen Turner, *Ella Enchanted* by Gail Carson Levine, *While No One Was Watching* by Jane Conly, *Protecting Marie* by Kevin Henkes, *The Watsons Go to Birmingham—1963* by Christopher Paul Curtis, *The Great Turkey Walk* by Kathleen Karr, *Our Only May Amelia* by Jennifer L. Holm, *Earthshine* by Theresa Nelson, and *The View from Saturday* by E. L. Konigsburg.

Look for stories with themes or subjects similar to yours. There will be some; don't let that discourage you. As you write, you'll fill your plot with your own characters and your own scenes. The authors of *The Long Winter* (Laura Ingalls Wilder), *Hatchet* (Gary Paulsen), *Island of the Blue Dolphins* (Scott O'Dell), and *Julie of the Wolves* (Jean Craighead George) each wrote about people fighting nature for survival, but the stories are completely different. The same reader can enjoy each one.

After you finish this book you may want to read other books on writing. The best tend to be short, such as *The Elements of Style* (William Strunk Jr. and E. B. White) and *The Craft of Writing* (William Sloane). As he talks about writing stories, Sloane never forgets the reader. Another good book for writers is both children's fiction and a joy to read: Randall Jarrell's *The Bat-Poet*. His story beautifully evokes both the work of writing and the difficult, sometimes uncomfortable business of finding an audience.

A number of books, both old and recent, thoughtfully explore children's literature, and there are also many helpful guides divided by literary category, age of reader, and subject matter suited to reader interest or special audiences. It's worth searching out—in libraries, bookstores, schools, on the Internet—those that suit your needs.

In addition to helping you locate books and articles about children's fiction, the Internet can link you to many resources about writing and about getting your book published. Web sites frequently disappear and can vary greatly in quality, but here are a few useful, stable sites you may want to consult: the American Library Association, <http://www.ala.org/parents>; the Children's Book Council (see also the appendix), <http://www.cbcbooks.org>; The Purple Crayon, <http://www.underdown.org>; and the Children's Literature Web Guide, <http://www.acs.ucalgary.ca/~dkbrown>. Your local library may have an active site or be able to recommend other useful sites.

Reading reviews is a good way to keep up on what children's

novels are being published and by which publishers. Several magazines devoted to children's books are particularly valuable resources, including *The Horn Book,* the American Library Association's *Booklist,* and *School Library Journal,* all of which publish both reviews and articles about children's literature. *The Bulletin of the Center for Children's Books* consists entirely of reviews, while *Publishers Weekly* includes children's book news and reviews.

Other good resources are children themselves and children's librarians, teachers, bookstore clerks, and friends, any of whom may be able to suggest good novels and be eager to discuss them with you after you've read them. You might also want to become familiar with other kinds of children's literature, including poetry, folklore, and nonfiction, as well as the lively, inventive books for beginning readers such as Dan Greenberg's cheerfully wacky Zack Files series.

Collect lists of children's novels and authors. Make a list of the ones people recommend, noting who told you to read them and why. Check out a pile of books you've never heard of from the library and search for treasure. If you don't find it, this is a chance to see why some novels, even published novels, don't work.

Start a list of the children's novels you read and add brief notes, with page references, about specific passages that interest you and might serve as models for your work: a bright description, a bit of subtle humor, the way the passage of time is conveyed, a lively transition between scenes, a tricky way of handling point of view.

Other writers' manuscripts are useful reading for any writer. Stories in progress, open to change but in which you have no emotional stake, are raw material for productive thought. If you can, find or start a writer's group or trade manuscripts with someone. Talking with colleagues who are clear-eyed and vocal may help you learn how stories work and how they can be improved. Better than abstract comments, specific instances drive the points home.

Read.

Exercise

Reread a children's novel you love, or read one that you've heard is wonderful. Be aware of yourself as a reader. Are you intrigued, excited, bored? When? Why?

Be aware of the writer behind the words. What has the author done to make the book so good? Where does the author disappoint you, perhaps with a word or by letting an action fade away?

Everything in a novel was put there by a person who could have left it out or told it in a different order, in a different voice. As you read, consider why the author made certain choices. Ask yourself what comes next—or what *could* have come next. A story may seem inevitable, but it's not. A story is as it is because some (one) person wrote it so.

The First Exercise Based on Your Story

> [T]he nearest anyone can come to finding himself at any given age is to find a story that somehow tells him about himself.
>
> —Norman Maclean, *Young Men and Fire*

This exercise should help you know your story better, thus helping you to work with it more effectively. In a sentence or two, describe the children's novel you plan to write. Do three versions, as if for three different people. You're writing your story for each of them.

1. The first person is yourself. What is it about the story you're working on that interests you and compels you to tell it? What was the first inkling of the story that attracted you?

2. The second person important to your book is a potential

editor or agent. How can you best attract the interest of a busy professional? Write a succinct description of your story as if introducing it in your submission letter.*

3. The third person—though not third in importance—is a child. Imagine that your novel has been published and a child has just finished reading it. The next morning on the school playground, she enthusiastically urges her friend to read it. What does she say about your story?

Keep these descriptions to remind yourself that all three people are important to the success of your story. As your understanding of your story changes, you may want to change these descriptions as well.

At moments when your writing is going badly or your energy flags, the first description can help you get back to your story's core. These sentences may express the story's theme. One writer I spoke with called this the "author's vision."

The second description is likely to include something about character and setting. Editors like an interesting, appealing central character in a new and intriguing situation.

The third description of your story will probably be centered on the plot. What is a story but . . . a story? Ten to one the child on the playground will tell her friend, "It's about this kid who wants to . . . , who jumps into . . . , who finds a . . . , who wins a . . . !"

Another useful succinct version of your story is what you tell someone else about it. If a person asks you what you're writing about, it's quite reasonable to say that you don't want to talk about it yet. Especially in the early stages, while you're first learning your story, it will seem as though you're telling your-

---

*See the appendix for more about publishing your novel. You must decide for yourself whether it's realistic or destructive to keep the marketplace in mind as you write.

self a fragile, precious secret, and you may want to keep it to yourself. But if you do answer the question, listen hard to what you say. Did you use any of your three versions to entice, to amuse, or to impress your listener? Did you add something new? What *is* your story about?

PART ONE

Tell Me a Story: On Plot

ONE

Beginning, Middle, and End

Every story has a beginning, middle, and end.
—Mrs. Baxter, my fifth-grade teacher

Fiction rests on three posts: plot, characters, and setting. Much of the pleasure in reading lies in the working out of the plot—arousing our curiosity, our hope, our apprehension; surprising us; ending in satisfaction. Yet the plot, just driving the story well from beginning to end, is often the greatest problem for both new and experienced writers. So it makes sense to begin here, with plot.

When, at the age of ten, I first heard the beginning-middle-end description of story structure, I resented being told something at once so obvious and so unhelpful. Much later I learned to understand the phrase in a way that has become a touchstone as I write.

In a combined fourth-/fifth-grade class I taught, I found that the boys (yes, always the boys) wrote stories of unremitting violence, consisting of one bloody action after another. Conversations with their teacher led, fruitlessly, to the larger culture. Since my involvement with the kids was limited to teaching writing, I looked for a literary solution.

Literature offered the truth that violent stories are as old as *The Iliad,* as old as the Bible story of Cain and Abel. Forbidding or denying violent stories made no sense.

So I began to ask the boys why. Why did he blow the other guy away? Why did he dig up the mummy's grave? Why did he keep vicious dogs in his basement? Not, What was his motivation?

but, Why? What inside him made him do it? What incident set him off? The boys had answers. Your story would be more interesting, I told them, if you write that, if you explain why your characters did what they did.

Next I asked, What then? Did the guy live? Was anyone else hurt in the blast? What did the killer's family do? The boys had answers here too. They knew what the consequences of the action might be.

They thought about "Why?" and "What then?" and wrote the answers into their stories, giving them shape. Some of the boys sensed that they had written whole stories now, and they were pleased. Sometimes, within the new, more human context, the ferocity of the violence became somewhat muted.

What happened here? The boys' first stories were all middle, all action. With no beginning and no end, they called forth from the reader no feeling for their characters. The stories had no meaning. People make choices and act because they're motivated to do so, and their actions have consequences for the people involved. It's important to include all this in a story.

Could the song "Frankie and Johnny" consist of "Frankie shot her man three times in the back" without ever mentioning that "Frankie and Johnny were lovers" or that Frankie "saw her man making love to Nellie Bly" or, later, that "'the bullet hurts me so!'" or that "Frankie walked up to the scaffold"? Although the boys had been proud of the violence they were able to deliver, their first stories weren't satisfying the way a well-made story is satisfying. With all middle, they weren't really stories.

Since I learned that lesson, I've recast beginning-middle-end as motivation-choice/action-consequence. This structure is a useful guide in thinking about what you want to write and what you've already written, about the entire story and the individual incidents within it.

The sequence may be repeated many times in the course of

a novel, whether it's a straightforward story of one character's struggle, such as *Stone Fox,* or a complex story that's rich with supporting and contrasting subplots, such as *Roll of Thunder, Hear My Cry.* Many fine novels consist of a series of episodes that has a cumulative effect. In such novels, each chapter may be a drama unto itself, closing with a satisfying sense of completion. These novels make good bedtime reading for younger children. Examples are Eleanor Estes's Moffat stories, the earlier Laura Ingalls Wilder books, and Beverly Cleary's Ramona books.

Motivation-choice/action-consequence calls forth the ancient and powerful sequence of an individual dealing with adversity. This is not a rigid formula to be applied at every point. The value of the words is in reminding the writer about the human experiences within a story. It is for the human experience that we write and read stories.

My tale of the fourth-/fifth-grade boys I taught, for example, makes clear my own motivation, what I decided to do and did, and the outcome for me and others. Telling the why and the what then brings life to a central action that would seem meaningless if considered alone.

Yes, Mrs. Baxter. Every story *does* have a beginning, middle, and end.

Exercise

Look at one of the smaller incidents of your plot. When and how is your central character motivated? What choices for action does he or she make? Where does the character feel the consequences?

Look at another incident. Practice being aware of this sequence.

There may be many of these sequences in a story. One may end as the beginning of another. For instance: Coming to the locked castle gate, the prince puts on a humble woodsman's clothing, fooling the gatekeeper, who allows him in. Then, still shabbily dressed, he meets his lady love in the great hall. What will he do now? The consequence of one action turns into the motivation for the next. Action creates the need for new choices. As one scene grows out of another, these building episodes give momentum to the story.

TWO

Structures of Hope

> The child is the hope of humanity. If they are going to change the world, they have to start off optimistically. I wouldn't consider writing a depressing book for children.
>
> —William Steig, qtd. in Anita Silvey's *Children's Books and Their Creators*

> [T]he form and structure of fairy tales suggest images to the child by which he can structure his daydreams and with them give better direction to his life.
>
> —Bruno Bettelheim, *The Uses of Enchantment*

Adults who are just starting to write often don't seem much interested in the middle of the story. They may have no real sense of how to get from the lively start they have in mind to the glorious ending. The middle—the very part that so attracts the child writer—they'll say almost dismissively, shows how "in a series of trials the heroine learns . . . , she grows . . . , she overcomes . . ."

What trials? This dismissal avoids the heart of the story: *how* the heroine learns, *how* she grows, *how* she overcomes. Perhaps adults slough off the middle action in their fervor to reach the end, to present the story's meaning and solution. But just as a middle has no meaning without a beginning and an end, so there is no story in bare motivation and consequence without the choices and actions that connect them. The sustained struggle of

the heroine—her choices made and actions taken—is the core of
the story. The center of the plot, where a reader's raised expectations
are met or thrillingly confounded and sent off in a new direction,
is much of what makes a good story so enjoyable. In that sense
the fourth-/fifth-grade boys mentioned in chapter 1 were right.
As readers identify with the central character's actions, his or her
struggle becomes their own lasting hope.

Satisfying plots require change: movement through incidents,
growth, a crescendo, a climax, and believable reasons and out-
comes. A good story requires tension or conflict, pressure and
counterpressure. Plot is movement.

One common problem among even experienced authors is a
lack of forward motion once the hero is set on his quest. Many
authors introduce one trial after another in no building sequence,
so that the quest bogs down in an accumulation of unweighted,
almost random incidents. This might be an accurate picture of
real life, but fictional drama must be controlled so as to give a
sense of momentum toward a climactic event. Unless there's a
strong underlying drama, in addition to momentary pleasure, stories will consist of "And then . . . And then . . ." and grow tire-
some.

In *The Wonderful Wizard of Oz* the resourceful Dorothy,
finding herself in a faraway, fantastical place, sets out toward a
crucial goal: getting home. In the story's middle, she meets characters who join her and help her overcome various obstacles.
Although some of her confrontations with strange Ozian populations come in random sequence, for the most part the reader feels
mounting tension, as the solution of one crisis leads to another.
Dorothy reaches the Emerald City only to be told that she must
go west and kill the Wicked Witch. She does this, returns to the
Emerald City, discovers the Wizard is a humbug, and misses her

ride back to Kansas. Again she sets forth, to see the Good Witch of the South. This time, after a few final bumps in the road, she's on her way home.

Someone telling a story to a friend isn't likely to have a static midstory. A story*teller* usually has the end in sight as she or he begins and keeps an eye on it while moving forward, incident by relevant, incremental incident. A storyteller's other eye may well be on the listener, whose responses make plain when the story sags or is unclear—when it needs adjustment. As a story*writer* you can make use of these tools. As you write the middle of your story, particularly, remember your end. Remember your audience.

Imagine Rudyard Kipling telling "The Elephant's Child" to his best beloved and the neighbors' children. As he talks he watches for roving eyes and restless bodies. He works to entertain his listeners at every moment with his rich, lively sentences. Yet all the time his story is moving toward its end.

At the start, the Elephant's Child asks "his tall aunt, the Ostrich, why her tail-feather grew just so, and his tall aunt the Ostrich spanked him with her hard, hard claw." At the end, when the Elephant's Child returns from "the banks of the great grey-green, greasy Limpopo River" with his long and useful new trunk, Kipling gives us the satisfying outcome: "Then that bad Elephant's Child spanked all his dear families for a long time, till they were very warm and greatly astonished. He pulled out his tall Ostrich aunt's tail-feathers."

The music of the words is wonderful, the family dynamics are funny, vicarious revenge is delightful, but it is the *center* of the story that we remember, the part that comes between starting off to satisfy a "'satiable curtiosity'" about the most dangerous possible question—"What does the crocodile have for dinner?"—and returning home triumphant.

In the center, the Elephant's Child gets himself into deadly trouble and staunchly, literally, pulls himself out. He resists when the crocodile snatches him by his lump of a nose, setting his hefty legs and pulling backward for hours to avoid becoming the crocodile's dinner himself—and thus creates his new trunk. During this contest, the audience at Kipling's feet no doubt grows silent and still. Hang in there, O Elephant's Child! Later, when he smites his elders, the listeners can share in the joy of a well-earned consequence.

You'll do well to build your midstory carefully, not as a random sequence of scenes, but as choices made and actions taken in moving toward the climax. The hero or heroine's committed, sustained effort, leading to a satisfying consequence, makes a strong story, a structure of hope nourishing for a child to read. In writing, as in life, it's often necessary to shore up one's sagging middle.

Exercise

Look at the middle of your story, where the plot is underway but events have not begun to climax. List the chapters or incidents. Do they have a logical, necessary order? Do they build on each other with increasing tension? Do they show the continuing struggle of the central character? Will your reader get bogged down in a series of interchangeable incidents or be drawn toward a compelling climax?

This study of your story is less an exercise than a necessary piece of work. Both as you plan to write and as you revise, it's important to take an unblinking look at the strength of your central section.

THREE

How the Reader Moves through a Story

The great sea-chest none of us had ever seen open.
—Robert Louis Stevenson, *Treasure Island*

[F]rom these dozen words I understood that the lives of all the honest men aboard depended upon me alone.
—Robert Louis Stevenson, *Treasure Island*

We often speak of a writer's readers. But just as writing is a solitary act, reading is a solitary experience. Ideally, one reads accompanied only by the story's vibrant characters. As you write, you may find it useful to think not of masses of readers or of a classroom of listeners but of one child, absorbed in and actively moving through your story.

An obvious but often overlooked aspect of writing is that the reader moves through a story at the author's direction. As you write, you're aware of the whole; your reader learns only what you tell, when you tell it, as well as whatever he or she can surmise.

The order in which material comes to the reader has a great deal to do with how it is understood. Consciously or unconsciously, a reader relies on narrative conventions to convey meaning, recognizing early who the hero is, for instance, or picking up hints about where the plot is headed. Particularly at the beginning of your story, a reader will be looking for signals, often quite subtle, to guide the way.

Thus, as you lay out your plot, you have not only opportunities to entrance the reader but also obligations. You're obliged to be mindful of what a reader knows at any point, to tell whatever will be needed to understand what's going on, and to earn the reader's trust and faith that you'll pay off on your hints and promises. You have the opportunity to use such hints and promises to involve each reader deeply in your story.

Authors create anticipation and interest through foreshadowing—preparing a reader subconsciously or indirectly for events to come. A reader will often *sense* that something is going to happen before he or she *knows* it will. From the first *Treasure Island* quote at the beginning of this chapter a reader may sense that something important will be found when that closed sea-chest is opened.

The endings of chapters and sections also can propel readers forward. You don't have to leave your hero hanging off a cliff each time, but it's a good idea to make sure they will want to continue reading, as Stevenson does in the second quotation. *Treasure Island* was written for serial publication, but in books, too, exciting chapter endings are often part of the pleasure.

You can keep your narrative moving by having your central character—and your villain, if you have one—actively working toward an end and by pointing out, over and over, directly and indirectly, where the story is headed. None of this precludes your changing course to surprise your reader—just take care to surprise in a believable way. You don't want a reader to suspect everything in advance but rather to be thrilled, as when it's a treasure map Jim Hawkins finds in that sea-chest.

Plot promises are one way to keep a narrative in forward gear. With the hero's situation growing steadily worse, a letter mailed in chapter 3 and still not received by chapter 8 may carry the reader's hopes and fears. The threat of a winter storm or preparations for a state fair can provide a dramatic timeframe for the action. A plot promise also can be quite explicit: in *The Jungle Book* (Rudyard Kipling), when Mother Wolf refuses to give up Mowgli, the "man-cub," for Shere Khan to eat, she tells the tiger that Mowgli will one day hunt him. It happens.

Such hints and foreshadowing, promises and payoffs, cliff-hangers and culminations play back and forth within a narrative, weaving together the parts of a good story. They help make it whole.

In *Stone Fox,* for example, the reader's curiosity is aroused by the first sentence: "One day Grandfather wouldn't get out of bed." By the end of chapter 1 little Willy is vowing to find out what's wrong and to do something about it. The reader becomes increasingly involved as nothing little Willy tries, such as harvesting the potato crop with a plow pulled by his beloved sled dog, Searchlight, solves the problem. Finally it turns out that his grandfather is despondent because he hasn't paid his taxes and the government is threatening to take away his Wyoming farm.

Helpful adults suggest that little Willy sell the farm. Instead, he enters a dogsled race in hopes of winning the large cash prize, though he's warned that the "mountain man, the Indian called Stone Fox," who has never lost, will also race. Little Willy is undeterred and practices with Searchlight every day.

To this point, the story is propelled by Grandfather's illness, the threat to the farm, and little Willy's high hopes and determination. The text hums with the hero's energy, and every chapter ends with a vigorous push forward.

Then, the night before the race, little Willy comes upon Stone Fox's five sled dogs resting in a barn. He reaches out to pat one— and is knocked down by a smack to his face. Little Willy explains to Stone Fox that he hadn't meant harm. He says he's not only going to race but he's going to win—and he tells Stone Fox why he must: "If I don't, they're gonna take away our farm." Stone Fox doesn't reply. As little Willy leaves, he tells the big Indian, "I'm sorry we both can't win." Alone, Stone Fox stands motionless, then gently pats one of his dogs. The reader begins to wonder about this man.

The reader's hopes for little Willy's victory are now burdened by a complexity foreshadowing a bittersweet climax. In some ways Stone Fox is a sympathetic figure. His motives are noble: he wants the prize money to buy back land taken from his tribe by the government.

Just before the race, Stone Fox's eyes seem to "lack the sparkle little Willy remembered seeing before." When the signal gun sounds, Searchlight springs forward, nearly tumbling little Willy from his sled. Stone Fox starts off dead last—and the reader senses that something unexpected will happen.

Well before the end of the race or the book, as he sleds past his house far in the lead, little Willy sees his grandfather at the window, waving him on, sitting up at last. It's clear that the climax will not be about Grandfather's recovery.

John Reynolds Gardiner, using a combination of crises, vows, cliff-hangers, and subtle hints, skillfully brings the reader through his story by building interest and tension. He pays off on his promises memorably at the end.

Such plot building takes careful work. For one thing, there's a danger in promising too much. Hints must, one way or another, come to fruition. In a narrative where nifty events forever seem in the offing and never happen, a reader may become exhausted with useless anticipation and lose faith in the storyteller. The author of a story told out of sequence must be particularly clear in tracking at every point what readers have been told, what they may suspect is happening, and what they're likely to be hoping for.

As a writer you need both to sense and to analyze consciously how plots will work for readers. Here are some ways to help yourself:

- Tell yourself other authors' stories when you're in the car, waiting in line, or before falling asleep. Follow the flow of information. Ask yourself, Why would I keep reading now? Do I know all I need to know in order to understand? Do I care? Why?

- Join a reading group and notice how people respond to published stories, what they look for, what they care about.
- Read plot summaries in media reviews of children's books.
  You'll get a sense of how plots move, or don't.
- Study genre books, mysteries, science fiction, romances, series books that depend on swiftly moving plots and clear narrative shapes.
- Be alert to plots. When your children tell you what happened in the lunchroom, when a friend tells you about a
  good movie, when your cousin says, "Remember when . . . ?"
  —be aware of the *story* being told. Why did your cousin remember that picnic?

Once you have a draft of your story, reading it aloud is a good way
to assess how—or if—the plot is working.

Exercise

Look over your outline, summary, or draft. At the end of each scene,
break, or chapter ask yourself if there's a good reason for your readers
to keep reading. There are probably small as well as large reasons (they
hope for another funny scene with the hero's goofy brother), immediate
as well as far-off reasons (will the teacher have her baby this week?),
specific hints and questions to which readers want answers (will the boy
in the orange coat turn out to be a bully or will he help the hero?). Put
yourself in your readers' place and ask, Do they have reason to care?

INTERLUDE: SECOND-PERSON STORIES

[F]eeling, not structure or ideas by themselves, is the power
that drives all good literature.

—Alfred Kazin, *Authors Guild Bulletin* (Spring 1998)

Do your readers have reason to care? Much of this book suggests
ways to encourage their intense involvement. In effect, the goal
is to write second-person stories.

One rarely reads a second-person story. Authors usually
choose between writing their novels in the first person, an "I"
speaking, or in the third person, as a story told about "he" or "she"
(see chapter 18). Yet we've all *heard* second-person stories, stories told about, and therefore to, "you."

One of the first second-person stories I became aware of was
by a boy in a fifth-grade class I was teaching. He read aloud a
speech given to a cowboy gang by the gang leader, a triumphant
recapitulation of the afternoon's work: "You rode to the back of
the bank and tied up your horses. Very quietly, you slid the window open and . . ."

The classroom was still as each of us became part of that
rough, tough robber gang. When the story ended, the author was
pleased, the class was thrilled, and I was ecstatic. "You wrote a
second-person story!" I told the poor, confused kid.

Later I realized that I'd heard second-person stories all my life
and that they'd meant a lot to me. This wasn't surprising, since
the ones I'd heard were all about me.

Second-person stories are usually old favorites with their audience of one. Often the storytellers are grandparents—masters
of this genre—though if we're lucky we have other sources, including aunts and uncles, high school and college friends, some-

one with whom we were in the military service, anyone who, long afterward, can remind us of who we were.

Good novels call forth the intense feeling of second-person stories. Recognition and identification are tools that have been used by authors since Homer sang of the Olympic gods and how they behaved—just like you and me and the neighbors. Children, particularly, love stories that seem to be about them, where the second-person feeling lures them in and binds them to the story's truth.

My mother once told me a second-person story about . . . second-person stories. When I was six or seven, she said, she'd taken me to see *The Skin of Our Teeth*, Thornton Wilder's play about cataclysmic events in history—the Ice Age, the Flood, war. Humankind was represented by a single long-enduring family: father, mother, son, daughter.

"What was it about?" my mother asked me afterward.

"A little girl," I said. "In the first act she plays with a dinosaur, in the second act she goes to the beach, and in the third act she has a baby."

I'd found myself in this play. It was about the fun I could have, the dangers I might face, and what I would do when I grew up. When this story of humankind's persistence and survival was first produced during World War II, audiences must have felt—indeed, hoped—that it was about them. Wilder wrote second-person stories for us all.

People making up stories to be published can hardly write of "you" to a thousand strangers. But they can write their first- or third-person stories to give the reader the intense, involved feeling of the second person. This happens not when a story is so general that anyone can step into it but when it's so rich in its specifics, in atmosphere, in feeling that it seems like our own familiar reality. While perhaps superficially unfamiliar, such a story can convey a deeper truth. Writers who work out of their own strong feelings for the characters and what happens to them beckon us to enter and be part of their story.

Children in another class of mine were working on stories about people of several generations. One boy read aloud his piece about a large family having breakfast before the children left for school. He described the mother serving food, hurrying each child along, fussing about homework, reminding, scolding, cajoling. Purrs of satisfaction kept rising from his listeners.

"That's just what they say!"

"That's how mothers do."

"My mother . . ."

"*My* . . . !"

FOUR

Using Summaries to Study Plot

> [A] tale shall accomplish something and arrive somewhere.
> . . . the episodes of a tale shall be necessary parts of the tale,
> and shall help to develop it.
>
> —Mark Twain, "Fenimore Cooper's Literary Offenses"

> Finally, books dictate their shape, form, content, weight, everything. They really tell you what they have to be. You just have to pay attention and listen to what the book is all about.
>
> —Maurice Sendak, *Publishers Weekly* (November 1, 1993)

One of the best ways to help yourself learn or feel the impact of your story as you work is, from time to time, to make and then study summaries of it. At first glance this may seem ludicrous.

Why bother retelling the story short when you're struggling to find time to write the long version? Why make a summary when you already know your story?

But how well *do* you know it? A summary may reveal a lot.

As writers, we work under a great disadvantage: we can't see our work whole. Since a story flows through time, comprehending it as a whole is impossible. Even to approximate such a view takes enormous effort.

I discovered this while visiting the studio of an artist friend. The canvas she was working on was in front of us. When we talked about any part of it, we could see how that part related to other parts, to the entire painting: this bit of yellow balances that other bit, the horse's legs parallel the line of trees, the boy's smile contrasts with his mother's frown.

"Thunderbolt" is not too strong to describe the force of my realization that I could never do this with my own work. I felt enormously deprived.

Painters, quilters, set designers, mosaicists—they can see all of a work at once. But writers, much like dancers, actors, and composers, may have a *sense* of a complete work, yet they can't *experience* it whole.

Look at Pablo Picasso's mysterious painting *Family of Saltimbanques* showing a group of itinerant entertainers standing on a vast, empty plain. Something is clearly going on between the man at the far left and the woman on the right. (X-ray analysis shows that Picasso painted the woman last.) As Picasso worked, he could readily see how each part related to all the rest, to the whole, and could use this complete vision to reinforce the sense of "something going on."

Imagine Picasso entering his studio and seeing at a glance everything he'd done so far on the huge canvas. Perhaps his eye was caught by the way the man's arms and hands make a series

Pablo Picasso, *Family of Saltimbanques,* 1905, Chester Dale Collection, © 2000 by the Board of Trustees of the National Gallery of Art, Washington, D.C.

of steps with the arms and hands of the little girl and the basket's handle and lip, all moving toward the woman. Perhaps Picasso then painted the woman's arms and hands also as steps but in reverse, blocking the motion with a stiff, upright arm parallel to the right edge. Perhaps he then painted the woman's flowered hat as a basket placed awkwardly on her hair, mirroring the child's basket of flowers, but upside-down. Such patterns of echo and opposition surely have to do with the picture's meaning.

Writers also move back and forth within their stories. A story has patterns, repetitions, connections, echoes, reversals among the parts. But moving from chapter to chapter, from page 17 to page 164, patterns may be hard to see, much less control. Part of your work as a writer is to learn ever more closely as much as you can about the story you're telling, to better imagine how a reader will experience it, then use that knowledge to reinforce the patterns in your material and weave them into a unified whole. But how do you do that when it's impossible to experience the sequence of events you're writing about all at once?

After the shock in my friend's studio, I searched for a way to gain the advantage that painters have. The best method I've found is to set aside my story and write and study a series of plot summaries—not the abstract meaning or the theme of the story, but the story itself. I write simple, concise, concrete reiterations of what happens, from beginning to end.

I may write these plot summaries as I'm preparing to start my first draft, as I'm writing the story, or as I'm revising it—whenever I need to think about the story as a whole and sense the balance and connections among its parts. A summary can mimic the forward momentum of a narrative, giving a sense of its driving force. Writing and studying these summaries help me to see how the story flows, how the parts fit into and feed on and follow one another.

Summaries can be from one sentence to several pages long. One-sentence and one-paragraph summaries—such as those suggested on page 15—are like the flap copy on a book jacket, except that they carry the story to the end. They help you hone a clear statement of the essence of your story. You'll find brief sample summaries at the beginnings of chapter 8 and the interlude following chapter 14.

For me, the most useful summary is two pages long, single-spaced, often with one paragraph per chapter. With these two pages in front of me on the table, my eye can flicker over my story, as over a painting, forward and back, up and down, across, moving quickly from part to part. This seems the closest I can come to seeing my story whole.

In writing the detailed summary of *Stone Fox* that appears in chapter 3, I learned how the focus and complexity of the story changed and deepened after the confrontation between Stone Fox and little Willy. Coming to such an understanding via a summary might help you to reinforce dramatic changes in your own story.

Although summaries are crude, straightforward renderings with nothing like the more subtle qualities that make a story appealing, by using them you may discover patterns and images you didn't know were there. Using extended summaries may sharpen your sense of what the reader, moving through, will need to know.

As well as being a useful tool for the orderly, editorial side of a writer's job, writing plot summaries can also stimulate the imagination and intuition. Summaries can convey the emotional thrust of a story, and in the flow of writing one you may find yourself creating new descriptions, scenes, or surprising qualities of character. You may discover a perfect word.

Once you've written a few summaries of your story, it pays to study them and the differences among them. You may discover that you've changed a sequence or left out an entire incident—and that this new way improves your story. In reading over my summaries of one manuscript I discovered recurring hats; in another it was dogs; in still another, photographs. What was going on? The subconscious has a way of slipping things in, of announcing a theme through repeated imagery. The meaning may burst upon you or it may take real work to figure out why some images seem to belong there. Once you understand your story better, you can control it better, using anything you've learned to your story's advantage.

During revision, studying a spread-out two-page summary should reveal the structure of your story and guide you in cutting and shaping it. You may discover hidden elements, a weakness in the middle, three chapters that would work better as two or in a different order. You might mark the names of important minor characters in different colors on the summary pages to track their movement through the story. Will the reader be adequately prepared for a new development—say, the cat who makes a crucial appearance late in the story? Use your summaries to systematically check out transitions, trace motivations, watch your themes play through the whole. This is a shortcut for learning what you're actually conveying to your reader, as opposed to what you think or hope you're conveying.

Working with summaries may be especially helpful if your story includes flashbacks or moves from place to place, or if you have a draft that didn't come from an outline but just spilled out. If your story moves on several fronts—hero and villain moving inexorably closer—or has various subplots, a summary will help you keep track of what's going on. Summaries are useful in writing an episodic novel, where the chapters are loosely connected to cumulative effect.

Telling a concise version of your story aloud, possibly into a tape recorder, is another kind of summary. Better yet, find someone to listen to you tell the story. Apart from the value of his or her comments, telling your story to someone will make you acutely aware of what your reader knows, what he or she needs to know and when. As you narrate, keep track of any changes you make.

If advance planning is not for you, you may want to put off systematically studying your plot until after you've completed a first draft and then try writing several summaries in a row. Writing, like all art, requires shaping. If you trust your subconscious to do this work, fine—but it might be a good idea to check.

Exercises

If you're just getting started, write down the story you have in mind from beginning to end in a single paragraph every day for a week. Be sure to give a clear sense of the specifics in the middle. Don't worry that the paragraphs are different each time—that's your mind at work.

If your story is well under way but you sense you have a problem, write it from beginning to end in no more than two single-spaced pages every day for a week. Write it from memory or use your outline (if you made one) to check whether your plan has resulted in a smoothly flowing tale.

If you've already completed a draft, do a week of two-page summaries entirely from memory. Divide the summaries by chapters or write a simple narrative. Take notes on every idea and question that pops into your head.

Then, or much later when you're in difficulty, study these summaries. Figure out what's missing, what's been added, what's changed from one summary to the next and from the actual story. Would using any of these changes make the story stronger? Do you get a sense of the story's momentum, of complex changes in the central relationships, of the ending's inevitability?

FIVE

Using Summaries to Solve Problems

> Originally I didn't want them to be wild "things"; I wanted them to be wild horses. In fact, the original title was *Where the Wild Horses Are*. The dilemma arose when it became obvious that I couldn't draw horses. So I had to think of something I *could* draw. Because the truth about the creative process is that it's a hard-line, nitty-gritty business of what you can and cannot do.
>
> —Maurice Sendak, "Visitors from My Boyhood"

> Imagination and intelligence have to work together. As soon as one or the other gets the upper hand, all is lost. There is nothing to do but throw away what you've done and start over.
>
> —Leo Tolstoy, qtd. in Henri Troyat's *Tolstoy*

It takes time to write, to sense what works and what doesn't, what you can and cannot do. Summaries of your story can be shortcuts for solving specific problems, for trying out alternative choices, for focusing on areas that need work. Summaries are like an artist's sketchpad: a place to try out an idea on the quick.

For example: If your central character keeps fading, watching while others take action, write a summary that focuses entirely on the *active* structure of his or her story. At every point, be aware of what that character is hoping, fearing—and what he or she is doing about it. Prod the character if you have to, to get him or her to jump into the action, and if this works, use the same prod in the story.

If you're having trouble keeping your narrative in forward motion, summarize each chapter or section of the story in a single paragraph. Then study the summary to see whether at each pause the reader has good reason to pick your book up again. Does something happen in each chapter to move the story along?

If you don't know whether to do this or that, write two summaries, one this way and one that way. This technique helped me when I was writing a novel about a girl and a dog. The story took place mainly on the street and in school, and the girl's family functioned simply as a home base for her adventures. While giving her only one parent would simplify the narrative, I wasn't sure that was best for her story. So I wrote two summaries, one with one parent and one with two. They immediately made it clear that if the girl had only one parent, her relationship with the dog and her need for it were differently charged. My choice was easy.

If you don't know whether to tell your novel in the first or third person, a good way to help yourself decide is to write the opening chapter each way. You can also write summaries in each voice to see which is truer to your narrative. Summaries would also help you determine whether or not a first-person narrator could know enough to narrate every scene.

If your central character seems two-dimensional, you might write a summary in which you change his or her gender as well as whatever follows from that. (Not for good—this is only an exercise!) You may discover some additional, more complex qualities for the character's personality.

If you sense that an unexpected subtheme lurks in the story— say, many secondary characters are motivated by greed—writing a summary focused on that theme can help you decide whether to enhance it or tone it down. A thematic summary may reveal more and different facets of the story and suggest how you might bring them under conscious control.

The beauty of using summaries to try out solutions to problems is that whether or not you wind up liking a new idea, you've only spent a few hours on summaries, not many days on a whole new draft.

Exercise

Think of a problem you're having as you prepare or write or revise your story—say, whether the main character's traveling companion should be a boy, a girl, an old woman, or an old horse. Write a summary using each of your options. Or free your mind to try a completely new alternative, taking a flying leap from the hero's initial motivation. Chances are you'll quickly find out that even though the story could be written in several ways, for you, for your characters, there's really only one way it can be.

SIX

On *Not* Planning Ahead

> A man who is not born with the novel-writing gift has a trouble-
> some time of it when he tries to build a novel. I know this from
> experience. He has no clear idea of his story; in fact he has no
> story. He merely has some people in his mind, and an incident
> or two, also a locality . . . and he trusts that he can plunge those
> people into those incidents with interesting results.
>
> —Mark Twain, *Those Extraordinary Twins*

> I don't bother with charts and so forth. . . . I don't believe the
> writer should know too much where he's going. If he does, he
> runs into old man blueprint . . . old man propaganda.
>
> —James Thurber, *The Writer's Chapbook*

> . . . I start Chapter One with rarely a notion of the story that's
> about to unfold. It's like wandering into a pitch-black theater
> and groping around for the lights. One by one, the spots and
> footlights come on, catching a character or two against a paint-
> ed backdrop. I sit back and enjoy the show. . . . I am not alone
> in these bungee jumps into the unknown. Both Jill Paton Walsh
> and the late Ellen Raskin told me they work the same way. . . . I
> don't know how one could write comedies, as I do, without the
> high wire of improvisation.
>
> —Sid Fleischman, qtd. in Anita Silvey's *Children's Books and
> Their Creators*

All my experience as a writer and teacher points to the importance
of prewriting planning about where a plot is headed. Planning
about characters, setting, and any aspect of a story can be useful,
but the lack of planning about plot seems to create the most problems for new authors.

Writing and studying plot summaries or chapter-by-chapter plans can help you know your story better and identify weaknesses early, when they're easier to fix. Part of your job as a writer is to organize your story for clarity, smoothness, and accessibility as well as for pleasure and dramatic effect. When the underlying structure is solid, the solutions to problems of motivation, sequence, and transition can be found *within* the world of the story. You won't have to carpenter them on awkwardly from outside.

Yet all this analysis of plotting may feel alien to the creative spirit in which you set out to write. In fact, many fine writers use far less planning than I've suggested. In effect, they simply let their stories pour out.

I've spoken with a number of these authors, and though each uses different words to describe his or her path, they all tend to start with little more than a sense of their story—a voice, an interesting character, a setting that they're curious about—then they feel their way as they write. One author ruminates until her story is worked out in her mind and then types it. Another points her hero toward a known end with no idea how he'll get there. Several authors say they feel less like creators of than conduits for a particular story; they say that their characters write their own scenes and dialogue.

Some authors feel that knowing too much about their stories in advance could be destructive. For those who rely on discovering their stories as they go, mapping things out might confine their imaginations and result in static prose. Following a plan might mean foregoing the richness that comes as they actively invent their stories. One author says that since so much of the progress of writing is in the doing, she urges beginners to keep going, to keep writing, to find out what's inside them ready to come out.

Accounts from several writers enlarge on these points.

Jacqueline Woodson, the author of *From the Notebooks of*

Melanin Sun, doesn't always plan her stories. She says she would be overwhelmed if she set out to put an entire multipeopled world on paper. Rather, she treats writing as a journey with a character—her job being to keep the character and herself moving forward.

Woodson's stories are grounded in emotional memories of her early teens. She begins by going back to herself at that age and remembering what it *felt* like. Starting with a character, without knowing what his story will be, Woodson puts two people in a room and conflict starts. "Plot happens," she says.

Beginning a writing session, Woodson rereads what she's already written and goes on from there. If a scene's moment and momentum have passed, she begins another scene. Only toward the middle of the novel does she begin to consider what is likely to happen and how her characters will feel about it.

Woodson knows she's reached the end of a novel when she writes a sentence and feels, Yes! This is what I meant to say in this story. Here's how she ends *Miracle's Boys,* in which three brothers who've had a contentious relationship are sitting on a stoop: "When Ty'ree started talking, his voice was low and even, like he was reaching way back to remember. Me and Charlie leaned forward, leaned into our brother, to listen."

Kathleen Karr, the author of *The Great Turkey Walk,* says she could never write plot outlines or summaries. She starts with a concept for a historical novel and researches it thoroughly, consulting detailed maps, old records, and writings from the period and visiting her settings. Karr finds that when her subconscious is saturated with material of this kind, as she writes it will come forth as a natural part of her characters' experience. She enjoys researching her novels and passes that enjoyment along, not as a lesson, but as fun for her readers.

Stories come slowly to Karr. She waits until she has the right first sentence and then she takes off. She says that by the end of the first paragraph she usually knows her central character but that the other characters arrive unexpectedly. "The truth of the story just happens" is how she puts it. Karr sets out knowing in general what her ending will be but not how her characters will get there, and she doesn't think of the ending as she writes.

At the beginning of each day's work Karr rereads the previous several chapters. This gets the story's voice into her head and gives her a running start into new work. She revises as she rereads, which means that her first complete draft is usually quite close to the finished manuscript.

Jane Conly, the author of *While No One Was Watching*, says she begins with a persistent voice in her head trying to tell a story. The voice, which she calls her strength, connects her to an emotional past. If the voice is compelling, she goes with it for the duration of the novel.

Conly has a good sense, from the beginning, of what her main character's transformation will be and the feeling with which he or she will be left, but she doesn't know how this will happen. She makes notes beforehand about the feeling of a story, about who the characters are and what they look like, and about settings— but not about plot. The ending she envisions functions as a pointer for her as she works. If the feeling and the voice are strong, she believes she can "patch up" any problems that arise.

Conly's process requires quite a bit of rewriting to braid together the various aspects of the story, to limit and focus it. She may have to throw out scenes or even a whole subtheme in order to tell her main story well. When she can't patch things up, or if the voice peters out, she must abandon the story.

Conly calls her method—some planning but mostly relying on the voice that tells her the story—"a luxury." She thinks it would be more efficient to know where she's going, and in fact she would suggest to adults who want to write that they plot things out. But she feels that in her own writing she doesn't have a choice. This is, simply, the way she works. Plotted-out writing, for her, turns out not to be true, and Conly's allegiance to truth has served her stories well.

For any writer there may be real pitfalls in working with a well-wrought plot in hand. You may control your work so tightly that your novel becomes lifeless, perfunctory. Each scene, instead of being an event in your characters' lives, seems written to accomplish your own purpose. Characters who exist only to propel a plot to its planned conclusion are generally wooden and uninteresting.

"Old man propaganda," to use James Thurber's phrase, is definitely to be avoided, whereas walking "the high wire of improvisation," as Sid Fleischman does, is definitely to be encouraged. But are these goals incompatible with careful planning?

Clarity in a story's development is important to you as you work as well as to your readers. Planning can help you to avoid false leads or building in "facts" that may prove useless or confusing. A story is much more than its outline, but readers depend on a strong, albeit fluid, structure to make meaning accessible. To rely on convention in plotting is not a weakness. Even a small child will sense a story's structure and depend on certain narrative conventions. If you don't pay attention at some point in your work to structure, to pattern and connection, to development, to how your reader will experience your story while moving through it, you may be just writing words and thoughts as they come into your head, not crafting a story.

Working within a strong framework can actually foster creativity. You'll be free to play, to invent productively, to take side trips without losing your way. Your story will be fresh *and* clear.

Although I plan carefully, I don't let my notes control the work as I write a first draft. Having used them to teach myself my story, I put them aside and rarely look at more than a single page of thoughts for each chapter so that my mind can play as it works. The notes then become resources, guidance for solving problems later as I revise.

Each writer must find his or her own way. If you're still discovering your best working pattern, you might acknowledge the value of both fly-by-the-seat-of-the-pants inspiration and careful preparation. Then, as you write and rewrite, you'll slowly find your place on the continuum from planning every detail of every chapter to complete improvisation. This isn't an either/or choice but a question of how much and what kind of planning works best for you.

PART TWO

People and Their Places:
On Characters and Settings

SEVEN

Someone to Spend the Afternoon With

> I realized that for all its sweep of history, the true narrative
> force of [*War and Peace* was] who gets Natasha.
>
> —Herman Wouk, *Washington Post* (May 16, 1995)

A psychologist who took my writing workshop made marvelous, insightful comments about the other members' manuscripts. (This only means, of course, that she often said what was on my mind.) When I mentioned this, she wasn't surprised. Many people who go into the field of psychology, she said, were literature majors in college. Both professions stem from an interest in human stories, in thinking through the dramas and patterns of other people's lives.

The engrossed child reader will care what happens to the central character in a story and will bond with him or her, with the character's adventures and struggles. As the character strives, perseveres, and achieves, the reader's satisfying connection with both character and story grows. Part of your work is to help this happen.

"Your characters," one reader told a writer, "are too accommodating to your story." In a way this was good news for the writer: she had written characters a reader cared about and would defend—even against their author. It was also bad news: the reader sensed that the writer was more interested in working out her plot than in the needs of her characters. How, then, to write rich, engrossing characters who seem to live in, not merely carry out, your story?

Children's novels tend to be about children and have a number of child characters. In most of them the central character is a child, often a warm, funny, interesting, brave, or otherwise appealing child. Many children's novels are about just *one* child; the other main characters are adults. This is true of such stories as Lewis Carroll's *Alice's Adventures in Wonderland,* Robert McCloskey's *Homer Price,* and Robert Newton Peck's *A Day No Pigs Would Die.* A few children's novels—*Mr. Popper's Penguins* by Richard and Florence Atwater, the various versions of the Robin Hood tale, *The Story of Dr. Dolittle* by Hugh Lofting, and *The Twenty-one Balloons* by William Pène du Bois come to mind—are entirely about adults, though it can be argued that the central adults in those stories resemble children. The same may be true of novels about animals, both humanized or realistic.

Readers learn a lot about the major characters in a novel, but the information they are given is far from all that could be said about a human being. You must know much more about your characters than you use directly in your story.

In preparing to write, it's useful to think about and perhaps list facts and qualities about your characters: age, family, family relationships, interests, spirit, goals, strengths, flaws, pleasures, dislikes, looks, pets, personal history, school, jobs, friends. How does she do in school? What does she do with her friends? What does she do when she's alone? Writing from a knowledge of such details can help to make a story feel real to the reader.

You must also know how and why the story you're telling matters to the people in it. What drives each character? How does each struggle to achieve his or her ends? Be clear about this yourself and convey it to your readers.

Once you've developed an understanding of your major characters—and you probably won't do this in a day or a week—it's helpful to write brief sketches about them, as if you were writing to a friend about someone you'd just met. Your list will prompt you, but let your mind move out on tangents, developing particularly qualities important to the story, such as a boy's on-again, off-again relationship with a friend or a girl's habit of daydreaming as she walks, so she often winds up lost. Sketches are a good way to ease yourself into writing about your characters. Lists and sketches can also be mined later on, when you need motivation for an action or your writing has gone flat.

The character sketches included in the Baby-Sitters Club series by Ann M. Martin are worth looking at. In each new book Martin introduces the club members to readers who don't know them, all the time keeping the story interesting for those who do. She does this by varying from book to book which of the girls narrates, each narrator telling about the others in an early interlude of several pages. The voice, the point of view, and the choice of what to include all seem fresh. Unfortunately, while this is going on, Martin's story stops cold.

A better way to handle character introduction or reintroduction is to avoid set pieces and show your readers what they need to know about a character's hat size, favorite breakfast cereal, or stutter as part of a novel's ongoing actions. J. K. Rowling reintroduces characters in later volumes of her Harry Potter series in new and interesting language as the story unfolds. Although there can be power in a well-written list (as we know from Margaret Wise Brown's *Goodnight Moon*), lists can be boring. Your narrative will move forward more effectively when such items are woven in as necessary parts of the story, sparking motivation or action, even the subject of small scenes.

Say, for example, that as L. Frank Baum contemplated a scarecrow character for *The Wonderful Wizard of Oz* he jotted down, "No flesh-and-blood needs." In the book he has the Scarecrow briefly explain this to Dorothy; then he shows us what this means in a lovely chapter ending. The Scarecrow and Dorothy, who is tired and doesn't like walking in the dark, come to a deserted cottage. Baum writes: "Dorothy entered and found a bed of dried leaves in one corner. She lay down at once, and with Toto beside her soon fell into a sound sleep. The Scarecrow, who was never tired, stood up in another corner and waited patiently until morning came."

Besides enjoying Baum's comic touch, readers now understand something about the Scarecrow. They are assured that Dorothy has met a kind friend and a worthy traveling companion.

A character's traits also can be shown indirectly, through the responses or actions of other characters. In the opening of *The Adventures of Tom Sawyer,* readers learn about Tom mostly through Aunt Polly's outrage and annoyance, which serve to make him highly attractive even before he enters the scene.

E. M. Forster, in *Aspects of the Novel,* divides characters into "flat" and "round." Flat characters, often minor and often comic, have one or two attributes with which readers soon become familiar. They are expected to play a variation on their theme every time they are present. The best writers—Dickens is famous for this—make even flat characters who have a single dominant quality seem real. Although they tend to fill a single niche and don't develop or change, flat characters can play important roles in a plot and can interest and please readers. Also, they're easy for both writer and reader to remember from scene to scene. You may find them useful.

Forster has much less to say about round characters, the "real" people who carry the passion of the story: "The test of a round character is whether it is capable of surprising in a convincing way. If it never surprises, it is flat. If it does not convince, it is a flat pretending to be round. It has the incalculability of life about it— life within the pages of a book." In other words, round characters are believably inconsistent—like most humans.

In developing the character of Tom Sawyer, Twain pulled off a number of convincing surprises. The boy, whom readers first meet as a rogue, in chapter 3 unexpectedly melts into a moon-struck lover, dazzled by a new neighbor, pressing her flower to his heart. Later, "full of pity" for the pain he is causing by letting Aunt Polly think he's dead, Tom kisses her while she sleeps. Of course he isn't so remorseful that he doesn't wait until his funeral to reappear; still later, back in rogue form, he tells Aunt Polly about the kiss in order to get himself out of a new scrape. In the crucial surprise, Tom takes the witness stand. Despite having twice sworn with Huck Finn never to tell what they saw in the graveyard lest they "Drop down dead in Their tracks . . . and Rot," he names the murderer, thus saving the falsely accused. Tom Sawyer is a wonderfully round character. (He is less so in *Huckleberry Finn,* where he tends to sing one comic note over and over. The roles of Tom in Huck's book and Huck in Tom's are worth studying if you're interested in character portrayal.)

Beginning writers sometimes feel their central character is the least interesting in the novel. This may be because in some sense we each feel we are the norm as, early in our lives, we believe our own family is the way families are. Therefore, as we are likely to identify with our main character from the inside out, however alien to or outcast from his world he is, he is simply me, known and so less interesting and peculiar than all those others.

Some authors try to solve the problem of ordinariness by loading their heroes and heroines with personality quirks. But quirks are no substitute for character. Initially amusing, a quirk has lasting interest only if it contributes to the story. We won't care about your hero for long merely because he wears his T-shirts backward.

Thoughtful telling about a character won't fully present her to the reader. More effective is to *show* her acting in a variety of situations. The reader wants to know what choices the heroine makes, how she responds to an emergency, what her sense of humor is like, and whether she's brave. You can meet a friend for a pleasant lunch every week, know how she dresses in every kind of weather, and admire her children's pictures, but you won't really know her until you've watched her deal with a crisis or, better yet, shared a crisis with her. Just so with a character. How your characters behave reveals their essence.

As you begin to write, even you won't know everything you need to know about your characters. Once you've done a first draft and seen them in a number of situations, you can go back and enrich the portraits in your early chapters.

From the start your readers should have a sense of what the central figure's struggle will be. If you can, show your hero or heroine in the first pages in a small scene—solving a problem, responding to sudden danger, making mischief—that demonstrates his or her character and foretells a larger quest. Then, as your story continues, new scenes will show commitment, humor, intensity, daring, cowardice, perseverance, bumbling, or resourcefulness to develop the character.

A character's struggle may be internal, interior—a common theme in young adult novels, where the most important development may be the character learning about himself. In his Nobel Prize acceptance speech, William Faulkner said that "the problems of the human heart in conflict with itself" can alone "make good writing because only that is worth writing about." Many conflicts rage in Mark Twain's *Adventures of Huckleberry Finn,* some brutal, some comic, but at the heart of the story is Huck's conflict with himself over how he feels and acts toward the slave, Jim.

Writers of fantasy have an obligation to make clear and believable any special powers their characters have. Demonstrating those powers early on or having other characters whisper about them with awe will reinforce the sense that they are real.

Finally, a word should be said in favor of villains. Think of how much two famous literary pirates, Captain Hook and Long John Silver, add to *Peter Pan* and *Treasure Island.* Hook is a flat character, a villain pure and very simple. Except for his comic pride in his high breeding—he's concerned about "good form" up until the moment of his death—Hook is nothing but vicious and brutal. When Peter Pan sends him overboard into the crocodile's jaws, the reader doesn't give him a second of pity. Silver, by contrast, is complex and ever changing, seductive to Jim Hawkins and also to the reader. He's out for his best shot at the treasure and at survival. He's smart, has great physical courage, and is infinitely treacherous. When he turns on Jim, the reader also feels deceived—yet fascinated. When Silver finally escapes—with some of the treasure—Jim is left with ambivalent memories, as is the reader. This villain is that interesting, that winning, that real, that round.

Whether flat or round, villains can be relied on to add to the reader's pleasure and add a strong element to the plot. If your story can support it, make your villain as active and as interesting as your hero.

Every jacket a character wears—how it's worn, its badges, the history of its rips and holes, what's in the pockets—offers a chance to portray that character. Without slowing the pace of your story, be aware of your opportunities and of your readers' satisfaction when people act in character—and when they surprise.

Exercises

Describe one of your characters doing something ordinary (drinking a glass of milk, climbing a ladder) as only he or she would. Every action, thought, and spoken word can be characterized and, at the least, should not be out of character.

Write a small early incident demonstrating, as if in passing, what will be an important quality of your main character: curiosity, kindness, or irrational fear.

Your story is part of the life story of every character in it. If you're having trouble making a secondary character come alive, try summarizing the entire story in the first person from that character's point of view. What does he or she believe is going on at various points? What are his or her motives for acting? Secondary characters probably see things differently from the main character. You may learn a lot about why your story happens as it does.

It's particularly useful to write a story summary from the point of view of an antagonist. Any conflict will be more interesting if you make the strongest possible case for the other side.

INTERLUDE: ONE MAN'S POCKETS

As you develop a list of your character's attributes, you may well wonder how much character can lie in a list. Here, to challenge your curiosity, is a list of some objects from one man's pockets: a pocketknife, a tiny pencil, two pairs of spectacles and their cases, a handkerchief, some favorable press clippings, a Confederate five-dollar bill.

What do you learn about the man from all that? That he's a little fussy? A little odd?

Hint: he was a real person.

Press clippings? He must have been important.

Yes. He was a U.S. president.

Lyndon Johnson? LBJ wore glasses but often kept them in his pocket. He was from the South. He was sensitive about his press. But isn't there something old-fashioned about those things?

Yes. They were found in 1865 in Abraham Lincoln's pockets after he was shot.

Probably you readily believe Lincoln carried these things. The concrete objects seem to evoke his reality. What do they tell you about him?

It's clear enough why Lincoln carried the spectacles, the pocketknife, the handkerchief, and the pencil: he needed them. He was flesh and blood. Perhaps he sharpened his pencil with his knife. Perhaps it pleased him, in the White House, to carry his own tool.

The press clippings? Lincoln had recently been through a bruising re-election campaign. Editorials and cartoons about him were often vicious. The election was in November, and he was killed the following April. He may have still liked to keep these kind words close by.

As to the five-dollar bill, a few weeks before his fatal trip to Ford's Theater, Lincoln had visited the Confederate capital of Richmond, newly captured by General Grant. Perhaps he got the money there. Perhaps, already pondering the difficulties of reconstructing the South and the Union, he carried the bill as a reminder of *all* the people his decisions would affect. Perhaps he wanted to touch something from a Confederate pocket.

The unexpected objects—newspapers clippings and Confederate money—may touch us most because they speak to us of Lincoln's struggles. Together the objects hint at who he was, both ordinary and mysterious—or to use Forster's term, a "round" character.

Exercise

List the things your central character keeps in his or her pockets, backpack, or secret hiding place. Consider hygiene, food, weather, money, contingencies, vices, amusements, defense, solace, curiosity, and newly found objects. Along with the ordinary include distinctive items. Add a surprise, even a mystery—something readers won't expect but will believe is there, something that "fits" your character.

You may want to muse on where the character has been lately, what he or she has been brooding about or hoping for in the days and week ahead. Unlikely items may foreshadow future choices.

When working on this exercise, let your mind go. Writers who think freely and imaginatively are often surprised by what they find in their main characters' pockets. You'll likely discover that you know more about this person than you thought you did. Note that this exercise is useful in learning about secondary characters as well.

EIGHT

My (Active) Hero

> Tony finds a silver whistle in the woods. He blows it and a bluebird appears in a tree, which instantly bears luscious peaches. Every day Tony blows the whistle, the bird comes, and the tree where it lands bears fruit. For Thanksgiving Tony plans to have enough fruit for everyone so he blows and blows the whistle. At first everyone is happy. But soon the whistle begins to blow itself, the bird flies from tree to tree, and more fruit falls than anyone can use. Tony throws the whistle into a river. He tries to chase the bluebird away, but it won't leave. The trees keep bearing fruit, which falls to the ground and rots. Finally, at dusk, the bird flies away. The next day the ground is clear of fruit and everyone has a wonderful Thanksgiving.
>
> —My brief version of a published story

> Jack slithered down the beanstalk with the Giant fast behind him. "Mother!" he cried. "Bring me my ax!" He jumped to the ground and grabbed the ax. He began to chop, and the beanstalk trembled. Jack could see the Giant's feet coming through the leaves above his head. He gave three more mighty blows, and beanstalk and Giant crashed to the ground.
>
> —My version of a scene from "Jack and the Beanstalk"

The bluebird and magic fruit story is interesting enough, but the climax is disappointing because the main character is ineffectual. The resolution is out of his control; it's no longer *his* story. Tony is a passive protagonist—more acted-upon than acting.

By contrast, in the action-packed finale of "Jack and the Beanstalk" everything falls (literally) on the resourceful Jack—and he emerges victorious. Both he and the reader are well satisfied.

An active hero makes for an exciting story. When the central character with whom readers identify chooses or learns to act on his own or someone else's behalf, when that struggle affects the progress of events and brings about change or improvement, then the reader feels satisfaction, pleasure, and hope (see chapter 2).

Conveying hope is more subtle than providing a happy ending. In the bluebird story the *action* has a happy ending, but since the hero didn't bring it about, since Tony was helpless as events unfolded around him, this is not a hopeful story. As with Jack's triumph or what little Willy achieves in *Stone Fox* or Dorothy's success in *The Wonderful Wizard of Oz,* hope is found where human efforts make things better. Hope can also be found in the growth of the heroine, in leaving the reader with confidence in her ability to act strongly and well, if not always successfully, as she goes off into the future.

The passive hero is a sad figure, like a child without choices— dismissed at home to watch television, ordered about at school, continually hauled here and there as an adjunct to adult activity. The active hero suggests that it's worth working at life.

So be careful to *keep* your main character working. When a story flags, it's often because the protagonist is sitting on the sidelines watching what happens, passively awaiting his fate. The effective force and energy come from elsewhere. A hero may well become tired or despondent at some point, as he may well choose a wrong path, but you should limit his absences from the heart of the story. Don't wait too long to pick him up and push him firmly back into the center of events.

This seems to me the central quality of good children's novels. Stories written for children traditionally have a sense of possibility: setting out, trying something new, overcoming obstacles. They show over and over that one can effect change, can make things better for oneself or someone else. Central characters who choose their own paths and take effective action are the engine of hope.

Exercise

What choices and actions by your central character bring about his or her final achievements or losses? Write a list of actions, large and small, or a summary that is entirely focused on your central character, perhaps beginning every sentence with his or her name. Try recasting your earlier one- or two-sentence summaries as a simple description of what your hero or heroine tries and achieves.

This exercise seeks to identify what your central character actually does, to describe spare and whole the character's active passage though the story. You may want to repeat the exercise several times as you write, to help ensure the character's momentum.

NINE

Setting = Where + When

> Halfway down the stairs
> Is a stair
> Where I sit.
> There isn't any
> Other stair
> Quite like
> It.
> —A. A. Milne, "Halfway Down"

As a child I resented, and probably skipped, any description of a story's setting that was longer than half a sentence. Okay, I'd say to myself, I know this takes place in World War II England or during a thunderstorm or in a cow's ear or . . . Now let's get on with the story! Even to the author, setting—the third post along with plot and character on which fiction rests—may seem less important, passive, merely there, a necessary stage where a story takes place.

But setting is far from just scenery. First, it physically contains the story, both grounding and challenging the characters. Second, the setting, any setting, from an ancient court to an eagle's nest, presents laws and codes of behavior that are the context for the story's action and meaning. (For a discussion of this second aspect see chapter 10.)

The setting is both the place where and the era when the story occurs and may in itself offer much of the story's pleasure. Children like to test their wings in new skies, over new lands, against new challenges. They like new vicarious experiences, perhaps as practice for when they'll be on a team themselves, or lost in a cave, or . . .

Place is usually some variant of home, school, or the Great Other, which is anywhere and everywhere else. Usually a novel is set in just one or two of these places. *Scorpions*, Walter Dean Myers's novel about a boy who becomes involved in a street gang, is one of the few stories I'm aware of that makes strong use of all three, giving a rich and vivid picture of one boy's world.

Using the Great Other as a setting—eliminating the familiar rigors of home and school, along with the authority of parents and teachers—has long been a happy choice for children's authors. It pleases readers to follow characters as they go off on their own or with some pals to the enticements of the wider world, from the wild woods of Jean Craighead George's *My Side of the Mountain* to the ultracivilized Metropolitan Museum of Art in E. L. Konigsburg's *From the Mixed-up Files of Mrs. Basil E. Frankweiler.*

Often the Great Other is a fantasyland, but even novels on as homey a scale as Eleanor Estes's Moffat stories, about the children of a widowed seamstress in a small town in Connecticut, explore the world beyond home and school. Jane Moffat, particularly, spends long hours out on the sidewalk with the Oldest Inhabitant or whomever, whatever, comes along. Some chapter titles hint at Jane's world: "Jane and the Chief of Police," "A Horse and Wagon," "The Coal Barge," and "The New Second Avenue Trolley Line" (from *The Moffats*).

Settings are *physical.* Making lists can help you mine the richness inherent in your settings. Try to be aware of the smells, sounds, sights, touch, and taste of places. Think about changes in the weather and the time of day. Such details will make your settings concrete, neither anyplace nor everyplace but the real place where your characters live. Dress your settings in all their trimmings: storms threatening, passersby smooching, animals running across the lawn.

Drawing detailed maps or diagrams of the settings as you plan and write will help you to fill out your story convincingly, to make characters move about smoothly and believably. Maps and diagrams will also help you to keep your facts straight.

It's best not to shove all you know about your settings at the reader in long paragraphs. A set piece of description can be boring and seems to place the setting apart from the story. Rather, keep your characters' feet on the ground by integrating the information into the ongoing story. When, as a scene progresses, characters are affected by wind and goose honks, headlights and bumps in the road, both they and the settings seem more real.

Mark Twain summed up the annoyances of setting descriptions in the introduction to *The American Claimant:* "No weather will be found in this book. . . . Many a reader who wanted to read a tale through was not able to do it because of delays on account of the weather. Nothing breaks up an author's progress like having to stop every few pages to fuss-up the weather. Thus it is plain that persistent intrusions of weather are bad for both reader and author."

Twain recognized that "weather is necessary to a narrative of human experience." To do his duty without interrupting his story, he quoted passages "from qualified and recognized experts" (e.g., "'It rained forty days and forty nights.'—Genesis") in an appendix from which the reader was invited to pick and choose.

For the ordinary writer, a more realistic solution is to involve the setting frequently, briefly, and pertinently with the narrative. In the following examples setting is effectively incorporated without holding up the story; the characters are present in almost every sentence:

> Neither of them spoke until they stopped on a circular driveway before the large building, so large its shadow cast a chill on their car and blackened the surrounding trees.
> "Well," Uncle Morris said. "Here we are." (Sylvia Cassedy, *Behind the Attic Wall*)

She looked for safety. An open field lay to her right. They could catch her there: they were not that drunk. Straight ahead was the river, but she could not swim. No one could. Water was for horses to drink and an occasional quick bath before weddings and such.

A sudden breeze rustled the leaves of a willow, as if it were calling to Beetle. Up she climbed into the branches, treed like a fox, waiting for what would happen next. (Karen Cushman, *The Midwife's Apprentice*)

Every setting—a kitchen, a ball field, or a castle—is actually a number of settings, and people occupy specific places within each. In the poem quoted on page 65, Christopher Robin is at home, but *where* at home? Halfway down the stairs.

When I've asked children to name places in their schools other than classrooms, they list thirty or forty places. For example: the little playground, the stage, the field, the roof, the gym, the principal's office, the teachers' lounge, the art room, the stairs, the locker room, the kitchen, the ramp, the bathrooms, the coat room, the library, the lunchroom, the lobby, the janitor's room, the secretary's office, the computer lab, the supply closet, the reading corner, the halls, the counselor's office. Any of these settings-within-a-setting would work well for the right scene.

The setting-within-a-setting that you choose depends on the effect you want to achieve. In *Treasure Island,* for example, Robert Louis Stevenson places the first conversation between Jim Hawkins and Long John Silver, whom we have yet to learn is the most dangerous of pirates, in the galley, the most homelike place on board the *Hispaniola.* Later Jim defends himself from partway up a tilting mast as a pirate climbs to attack; when Jim shoots the pirate, his body falls directly into the water. For anyone who knows the scene in which Jim—hidden but surrounded—overhears the pirates plotting, the simple words "apple barrel" evoke frightful memories.

Setting also involves time, the era when the story takes place: twenty-first-century rural Pennsylvania isn't the same as seventeenth-century rural Pennsylvania. You may want your story to take place in one location in several different eras. An extreme example is Peter Dickinson's *A Bone from a Dry Sea,* in which the story's two converging threads take place in a single setting, millennia apart. The crises of characters and their communities are each appropriate for their time.

The time of year during which your story takes place should be chosen with care. If the story lasts for several months, play it out in your mind or on paper from beginning to end in terms of weather. Times of day may be important, too, as may the calendar of an organization like a school or ball club. A school field day shouldn't come up in December unless the story is set in a warm climate.

Like a map, a timeline can be useful in helping you to keep the facts of your story straight. If you plan to tell events out of sequence, you need to be able to control what your readers know and when they know it. You may need two timelines: one for the actual order of events and the other for the order in which the events are revealed.

If you want to introduce large chunks of past events, Natalie Babbitt's *Tuck Everlasting* provides an interesting model. The two extended flashbacks are not presented early on, when they might be confusing or boring, but much later in the story, when readers are eager to understand what's going on. These aren't true flashbacks, in which readers are taken back to see early scenes for themselves, but instead are told in the present by characters who care about what has happened. Other characters eagerly attend, and the tales both clarify motives and point readers back into the story.

As you prepare your setting, do whatever research you'll need early on so that you won't weave factual errors into your plot. Even if you think you know your subject well, study it some more, submerge yourself in it, study photographs of your setting, visit it, interview people who know it. Be sure you're accurate about language, clothing, timing, habits—all the details that will make your story seem true.

If you're going to interview someone about an aspect of your story, it's best to learn as much as possible beforehand so that you won't waste interview time on what you can find out for yourself. Encourage the person to talk about the curious aspects of his or her job or hobbies or neighborhood, the odd or funny things that only an insider would know.

For my novel *Nightwalkers*, which had a "real" elephant character, I first read widely about elephant behavior. Then I spent hours watching elephants at the National Zoo, asking questions of the keepers, taking photographs and careful notes. I became so familiar with those elephants that I often could tell what one was about to do. Once I felt I knew the basic facts about elephants, I was ready to talk with the mammal curator, an elephant specialist, and ask questions pertinent to my story: Why, each time an elephant meets a human friend, does she smell him so thoroughly? What does it feel like to ride an elephant? How good is her aim when she throws? My questions called forth stories from his experiences, many of which, in some form, enriched my book.

People are enormously helpful when you tell them you're writing stories for children. They want to be sure you get their profession, their hometown, their history accurately. Both the curator and one of the zookeepers read two drafts of *Nightwalkers*, correcting me on elephant behavior—and sometimes on grammar.

Even though writing fiction gives you a certain license to invent and change, you'd do well to be accurate and realistic wherever possible. Keep careful records of your sources so that you can go back during the publication process to verify facts and quotations.

If your story occurs in a far-off time or place, say so early on. If you say nothing about where and when, readers will assume the story is set in the present, in a community much like their own. Give them a sense of the place even if you think it's ordinary: it may not be ordinary to them. Each community has its own ways.

A tour de force of setting is, literally, *The Monster at the End of This Book* by Jon Stone. This rare second-person book is a kind of *Tristram Shandy* for three-year-olds. The setting is the book itself; the time is whenever the book is read. The central character is the child listener-reader, who creates the story's action by turning the pages. A Sesame Street character, lovable, furry old Grover, desperately tries to prevent the child ("you") from going on ("Stop turning pages!") because he's read the title page and learned that there's a monster at the end of the book. Much about reading books is conveyed here, including the convention of the surprise ending. Guess who the monster turns out to be?

Exercises

Choose one of your settings and list all the possible settings within that setting: *where* in the stadium, *where* on the beach, *where* in the lab. Variety and detail, accoutrements of these precise places—the things characters pick up, slip on, fear—will help to give your story a sense of reality.

Next, bring a character into one of these places and connect him or her to it through a small action. If the action is in character, if it moves the plot forward, so much the better.

Name three places that only one character in your story knows about.

Make a map or diagram of a setting you'll use often. Mark the creatures and things your characters see as they move through it, first in one direction and then another. Make note of smells and sounds. Take your time and put in as many details as you can think of. As the cast of your story strolls through the setting, what do they do, where do they linger, what do they take away? Without slowing your story, make sure your settings are inhabited, not just backdrops for action. Use the map or diagram as you draft future scenes, and add to it as you learn more about your story.

TEN

Setting as a Context for Meaning

> This is a boy's lot: anything he does, anything whatever, may afterward turn out to have been a crime—he never knows. And punishment and clemency are alike inexplicable.
>
> —Booth Tarkington, *Penrod*

> [I]n a first-rate work of fiction the real clash is not between the characters but between the author and the world.
>
> —Vladimir Nabokov, *Speak, Memory*

Childhood is all about figuring out the rules and then figuring out what to do about them. Thousands of child Freuds may be asking this minute, What do grown-ups want?

The place and time of a story supply its cultural, social, political, and moral context. There may be several sets of rules and expectations that underlie the thoughts and actions of the characters. School, nature, religion, gang, holiday, grandparents' home—each has its own rules and customs. Without comprehension, conscious or unconscious, of this framework, the reader won't understand the story.

These abstract words don't necessarily imply anything deep

or complex. A custom that could be important to a story is that the children in this community, in this era, in this family, come home on time for supper. The reader should know this.

A story is about the choices and actions of characters within a specific context and situation. When Grandfather won't get out of bed in *Stone Fox,* little Willy's choices are contained in, and their outcome is in part controlled by, the setting: Wyoming is farm country and the potatoes must be dug. Wyoming levies taxes and they must be paid. Wyoming has heavy snows and there's an annual dog-sled race. Long ago in this area the white man's government took the Indians' homeland away.

To see how local values and customs affect meaning, try moving a story from the place and time in which it was imagined to another place and time. You'll find that more is changed than the scenery. Forests are the setting for Laura Ingalls Wilder's *Little House in the Big Woods,* J. R. R. Tolkien's *The Hobbit,* Gary Paulsen's *Hatchet,* and Rudyard Kipling's *The Jungle Book,* as well as much of Natalie Babbitt's *Tuck Everlasting* and A. A. Milne's *Winnie-the-Pooh,* but they're very different places and in very different times. The "law of the jungle" in *The Jungle Book* fits no other story. The woods in *Little House in the Big Woods,* set in 1872, and *Hatchet,* set in the 1980s (when the book was published), seem comparable but are separated by a century of change in both technology and family culture; the contexts of the characters' struggles to survive are entirely different.

Roll of Thunder, Hear My Cry is set in many places and involves overlapping and contradictory social codes. Like the children in the story, the reader must try to make sense of them all. Mildred D. Taylor opens her novel with the narrator, Cassie Logan, and her three brothers walking to school along a dirt road. When a busload of white children speeds by, the black Logan children scramble up the bank to avoid being sprayed with dust.

When they meet children from a white family that lives nearby also walking to school, readers begin to sense that this road is the heart of the Logan children's Great Other, the only place in the segregated Mississippi of 1933 where they regularly encounter whites without adults to set and enforce the rules. Much of the novel takes place on this dirt road.

Even a story set in an "ordinary" American family has its unique context of values and customs. What are the household spending habits? Are the kids allowed to play outside with neighborhood friends? Do the parents teach their children to use weapons or do they pull even toy guns out of their hands? Do family members tease each other? Do they instinctively support each other? Who buys or makes the presents? What are the rules for using the computer? What role do grandparents play? Who cuts whose hair? Who walks the dog? Answers to such questions provide the context within which, against which, the characters' stories unfold.

The intersection of a character's story with its social setting is one reason time-travel stories are so difficult to write well. If the characters go to a past that's familiar to the reader, then they can act out their own story and can themselves grow and change but they can't change history or in any way influence the reader's present. The lack of effect on their surroundings can make the story seem insipid or trivial.

In writing fantasy, it's especially important to be consistent about customs, laws, and everything else about the setting that has an impact on the characters. If you're making up rules for a magical world, be certain that they're integral to the story; extraneous rules are distracting. If the narrative voice accepts the rules of your setting, if the reader learns them as the central character does, this will encourage the reader's belief.

It's a good idea to make any special rules clear early on. Introducing a cloak of invisibility just when your heroine gets into a tight spot makes readers suspicious and leaves them feeling cheated. Beginning writers of fantasy often assume they can write anything into their story that they wish. Not so. While children love new systems, they catch on fast. Two or three quick fixes or inconsistencies and your credibility as a storyteller is lost.

A good example of how to use a magical device can be found in *The Wonderful Wizard of Oz*, when the old woman who is Dorothy's first friend kisses her, leaving a shining mark. "[N]o one will dare injure a person who has been kissed by the Witch of the North," the woman says. Much later, when the Leader of the Winged Monkeys is about to harm Dorothy, he sees the mark and motions to his followers not to touch her. Because Baum mentions the protective mark well before his heroine needs it, readers have the pleasure of anticipating its use; and when it is used, they believe.

Including a summary of a fantasy's special rules can be useful, as in this passage from Lynne Reid Banks's *The Indian in the Cupboard:* "As he had it figured out so far, the cupboard, or the key, or both together, brought plastic things to life, *or if they were already alive, turned them into plastic.* There were a lot of questions to be answered, though. Did it only work with plastic? Would, say, wooden or metal figures also come to life if shut up in the cupboard? How long did they have to stay in there for the magic to work?"

In *Tuck Everlasting* the fantasy depends on a coincidence: a number of apparently unrelated people decide to go to the same place at the same time. Yet Babbitt's skill in introducing her characters and in not revealing just how big a coincidence their meeting will be until she's well along allows her to ease readers into accepting the story, fantastical premise and all.

The broader context is invariably a factor in any character's story, but how much the character's actions and the story's events impact on the broader context varies from one story to the next. In a fairy tale where the prince saves a blighted kingdom to win the beautiful princess, his story affects the social framework. In E. B. White's *Charlotte's Web,* Wilbur is saved in the end, but the other farm animals apparently will be slaughtered according to the unaltered code of the farm.

In its simplest terms *The Wonderful Wizard of Oz* tells about a girl who finds herself in a fantasy world and struggles to return home. Yet clearly this book is also about political transition: who rules where is a constant preoccupation.

Like every fantasy world, Oz has its codes and practices, and Dorothy and the reader must learn them. Each quadrant of the country has a dominant color; whole populations are in one kind of trouble or another. While good witches live in the North and the South, wicked witches plague the East and the West. The Wizard is a fraud, ruling through sleight of hand. Many things, it turns out, are rotten in the land of Oz.

Dorothy's determination and courage help her and her friends and also attack political evil. The two bad witches die, the Wizard is exposed and flees, and at the end Dorothy's good-hearted friends sit firmly on many of the local thrones. Before she returns home, the little girl from Kansas has effected a complete political revolution.

The world of Klickitat Street in Beverly Cleary's Ramona stories also has its rules, expectations for behavior, and hierarchies of power. Ramona's friction with these—in her home, in her classroom, on the sidewalk—is often the basis for the story. Every bit as much as the land of Oz, Ramona's small world has codes that the spirited young heroine must learn and deal with as she's acted upon by powerful forces. But unlike Dorothy, who doesn't hesitate to challenge the rules that seem to her to be unfair or wrong and emerges a triumphant heroine to inspire hope in her readers, Ramona doesn't much affect her world.

When, impetuously or after careful thought, Ramona confronts unfair rules and situations presented by her family, school, and neighborhood, she rarely triumphs. Although she wins small victories that seem appropriate in the context of specific events, over the course of the eight books named for her, as she ages from a four-year-old to a fourth grader, she mostly learns how to compromise, how to simmer down. In the beginning, a charmingly exuberant Ramona gets into all sorts of trouble. By the end of the series, having learned how to accept and work within given boundaries rather than challenge them, she seems to have largely capitulated to the authority figures who surround her.

How characters respond to the rules and codes that govern their setting will often be the heart of a story, revealing much about a writer's theme.

Exercise

Make a list of the codes that are important to your setting, even if they're never stated explicitly in the story. Which ones are reflected in the behavior of your central character or are important to the choices he or she makes?

Probably several of these codes will be critical to your story's meaning. Pay attention to how they're introduced, developed, and played out. Is a clash between two settings a factor in your plot? Being aware of this framework should help you to understand the complexity of the characters' choices. Does the hero struggle to defy authority or to persuade authority to help him? Is he trying to defy the part of himself that has absorbed society's rules? Is he fearful of nature's laws?

INTERLUDE: SETTING AND CONTEMPORARY CHILDREN'S NOVELS

> The United States, democratic and various though it is, is not
> an easy country for a fiction writer to enter: the slot between
> the fantastic and the drab seems too narrow.
>
> —John Updike, *New York Times Book Review* (September 24,
> 1995)
>
> But what can he *do*? What could a kid really do?
>
> —A sixth grader, responding to a suggestion that the hero of his
> story should be more active

What *can* a child really do? It's hard these days, for a child—or
for a children's book author—to know.

Children like to form clubs. But often, after the name is chosen, unworthy others are excluded, officers are elected, a meeting place is prepared, and refreshments are consumed, the question remains, What is there to do? The strength of Ann M. Martin's
Baby-Sitters Club stories is that club members actually do something that matters.

Anyone who writes contemporary novels for children lives
vicariously in their world, and that world is getting smaller. The
"slot" (as Updike might say) for "really doing" (as that sixth grader might say) is getting narrower.

A junior high school teacher once told me, when I suggested
that stories might grow from having her students make maps trac-
ing their walk to school, that since most of them lived in the hous-
ing project across the street they didn't walk far enough to make
the exercise worthwhile. After school, she said, since the nearby
streets were so dangerous, most of her students went home and
watched television. They had, she concluded, few experiences to
write about.

I was appalled that the teacher had so little sense of her students as people with lives important to them and imaginations that could flourish. Yet it was also sad to hear, again, of children's circumscribed lives.

Many of today's children spend much of their time in daycare, school, and after-school programs. Their experiences—those delivered via television, music videos, computer games, movies, or music, or even active ones such as gymnastic or karate lessons, soccer practice, and whatever is on their daycamp schedule—are often shaped and controlled by others rather than by the children themselves. Children learn to accept this. I've seen them come into the art room, sit down and confidently paint a wide line of blue across the top of their paper and a wide line of green across the bottom, then wait for the teacher to tell them what, today, goes between earth and sky.

This confinement of body and imagination means that children spend less time in the Great Other, where they might initiate, browse, ponder, explore, and discover the raw material of their own stories. My niece, who loves what her own mind can do, put it this way: "When I watch TV it's the TV that's having all the fun."

Children's novelists are similarly deprived. Of course there are stories—good stories and good times—to be had in daycare, in after-school programs, and in organized sports. Family stories have been at the heart of literature since Adam and Eve. But home and school settings tend to offer up intensive, not expansive, plots. For children ages eight to twelve, the age that looks outward to the greater world, the literary family was once only the starting point. That breeding ground of heroes and heroines, the Great Other—the alley, the far side of the lake, downtown, the gang, even interesting strangers—was the center of all that mattered. Nowadays, the Great Other is less accessible to children and to the people who write for them. Authors must work harder to find and establish a believable Great Other for their settings.

The problem is not that families have changed radically. Families in the classic stories are often non-nuclear: Aunt Polly calls Tom Sawyer "my own dead sister's boy, poor thing," which is the last we hear of his birth family. Dorothy lives with grim Auntie Em and Uncle Henry. Mowgli lives with Mother and Father Wolf. The Moffat children's father is dead. Jim Hawkins's father dies (in chapter 3) partly of pirate-induced stress and is dispensed with in half a paragraph. The list goes on. No one dwelt on these situations; they weren't problems to solve or a limiting context for the stories. Rather, they were the givens from which the children went on, went *out,* to adventure.

Currently, in literature as in society, we tend to keep children contained. Many of today's novels for elementary school children show homes and lives dominated by troubling adult secrets. The dramas in these fictional children's lives stem from the adults' situation. The hero's work is to discover, then come to terms with, the secrets of the past. In most such novels there's little opportunity for a child to move outward.

Belle Prater's Boy by Ruth White is a good example of this. Beautifully written and involving, the novel is set in a complex community and revolves around a lively, interesting relationship between two young cousins. But the burden of the story is the mess that well-meaning adults have made of their family lives and how the children learn the various secrets and deal with them.

Discovering and facing parental shortcomings and woes used to be the work of adolescence or adulthood. Many stories now give this weighty task to younger children. Children I respect take on these novels with pride and deadly seriousness. In the eyes of the smart, well-loved young girls who have urged me to read such books, I see a touch of sadness. It's the deadliness of their seriousness that worries me. I wish they were reading *children's* stories, not reworkings of adult dramas through children's eyes.

Does it make a difference if we squeeze the Great Other out of children's novels and contain their stories in narrow places? Does it matter that we leave young Ben in front of the television, making sure he's watching a nature film, instead of letting him play outside, where he may have to decide for himself whether or not to touch a shimmery-green beetle?

To put it selfishly, Ben watching a nature film is not a promising start for a story. Ben on his own in his backyard, down the street, by the creek, working up the courage to pick up that beetle of shimmering green, could lead to an interesting novel.

No doubt children have always felt hemmed-in by adult rigidities and purposes, by institutions and schedules. But isn't that exactly why so many satisfying children's stories take place in the Great Other, where children find important things to do removed from the here and now to the there and then?

The tradition of getting away from the everyday life of school and home does not necessarily mean an escape into fantasy. Many beloved older novels are about children moving out into their own wider contemporary world: *Caddie Woodlawn* by Carol Ryrie Brink, *Homer Price* by Robert McCloskey, *Harriet the Spy,* by Louise Fitzhugh, *Johnny Tremain* by Esther Forbes, *Julie of the Wolves* by Jean Craighead George, *Island of the Blue Dolphins* by Scott O'Dell, *The Great Brain* by John D. Fitzgerald, *The Witch of Blackbird Pond* by Elizabeth George Speare, *From the Mixed-up Files of Mrs. Basil E. Frankweiler* by E. L. Konigsburg, *The Saturdays* by Elizabeth Enright, and *Summer of My German Soldier* by Bette Greene.

A number of authors have followed suit in recent works: Gary Paulsen in *Hatchet,* Nancy Farmer in *A Girl Named Disaster,*

Bruce Brooks in *The Moves Make the Man,* and Karen Hesse in *The Music of Dolphins.* Although the adults' past casts a long shadow in Cynthia Voight's *Dicey's Song,* it's what the children do now that matters. Jane Conly sends her child characters off into the wild woods in *Trout Summer* and along urban streets in *Crazy Lady!* to make their own choices and initiate their own actions.

Just as the thin, restricted stories found in most series books give children little of lasting worth beyond a pleasure in reading, a rich, expansive novel will enlarge children's experiences. One summer vacation when my kids were ten and eight, I read *The Adventures of Huckleberry Finn* to them. They needed some parts explained but enjoyed the story hugely, laughing and talking as we went along. The next summer I suggested we take with us another long read-aloud story. Immediately, eagerly, as if there were no other book in the world worth reading, my son said, "Read Huck Finn again!" "Yeah, Huck!" my daughter agreed. They craved to hear again about the wider world that Huck, master escapee from home and school, had shown them.

Are the changes I've described in real life and in many contemporary children's novels linked? It feels so. This is often our children's world: two working parents, single parents, violent streets, media-dominated homes and schools, scheduled or circumscribed "free" time. The point here is not to blame but to consider the effect on children.

Children long for models of effective action: "What could a kid really do?" Reading *Stone Fox,* we have no doubt little Willy can take on the momentous task of saving the family farm. But really doing something is hard. It's just *because* children feel so little power that they need the hope that an individual—that they themselves—can act and accomplish.

If settings in children's novels are limited, surely this reinforces the limits in children's lives. Wouldn't it be better to give children stories in which child characters break out and do things—whether realistically or fantastically—for themselves? The challenge for children's authors is to help children imagine moving out of their constricted lives to make real choices and take effective actions. Otherwise, I fear, we may see the numbing of hope.

ELEVEN

Finding Children and Their Places

> When researchers [in a 1926 survey commissioned by the American Library Association] asked 36,000 children in 34 cities to name their favorite books, fully 98% responded by listing titles written by Edward Stratemeyer, the fabulously prolific—and to librarians reviled—author of the Rover Boys and Dave Porter series and publisher of, among others, the Hardy Boys, Bobbsey Twins, Tom Swifties and, starting in 1930, the Nancy Drews.
>
> —*Publishers Weekly* (July 1997)

> As a kid I had thought a lot like an adult. As an adult, I thought a lot like a child. In other words, I had really been pretty much the same person all my life.
>
> —Bruce Brooks, qtd. in Anita Silvey's *Children's Books and Their Creators*

Children's book authors must be aware of children as potential characters and as potential readers. Who are children? is an important question. How can a writer know?

Children are humans, quite like the rest of us, but there are some special concerns in writing for them or about them. Sometimes, when flying into a strange city, I look down at the jagged line of high-rises or the gentle arcs of suburban homes and think about the children who live there. Could I write about them and the places they know? Would they care about my story? Writing for children is not a matter of simply loading on the poop jokes or setting every scene on the baseball diamond or in the girls' bathroom. There were good reasons why young readers enjoyed the Stratemeyer series.

Writing for children means, above all, having a lively story to tell and an active central character to help tell it, as those Stratemeyer books, to their credit, did and today's popular series still do. Some other commonly accepted generalizations about what child readers want include:

- they want to have fun—with plot, incident, and language;
- they're curious about the world and attracted by an interesting setting, by incidents bearing news;
- they want to read about kids their own age or older (apparently boys are still more eager to read about boys, while girls will read about either sex);
- they like animal stories, witch stories, school stories, sports stories, realistic stories, fantasies, mysteries, characters in strange shapes with strange powers, characters just like them, and so on.

My sense is that it's most helpful simply to be aware that you *are* writing for children. Be aware of the age you're writing for, perhaps keeping a specific reader in mind as you write. To make certain that your telling of the story is on target, focus on your main character. If she's childlike, if she seems about right for her age, then the rest seems to fall into place. (For the mechanical aspects of writing for children, see chapter 20.)

Child characters can help give child readers access to a complex story. The fantasy *Tuck Everlasting* is almost entirely about adults and a serious, mature issue: the temptations of immortality. Yet Winnie, the child heroine, is never more than a child and never does anything a wise and brave child couldn't do. She invents, volunteers, and carries out her own part in the climactic action in a childlike way that is quite believable.

Be aware of the children around you. Almost too late I realized that my own son and daughter were . . . children. Luckily, a friend who wrote a weekly children's television show was stumped for an idea and phoned to ask if my kids had done anything interesting lately. The call opened my eyes. Immediately I took pictures of their rooms and for a month made detailed notes on their daily doings.

If there are no children currently in your life, find ways to get close to some. Write notes about your own childhood at the age you're now writing for. Who was in your class? Who was on your team? Who lived next door? Describe some of these people. What was your room like? How was breakfast eaten in your house? How did your pet smell? Write down as many details as you can remember. If you can't remember many, or even if you can, ask your parents or siblings or childhood friends to tell you more.

Look through books of photographs of children and their families; look through your own albums and school yearbooks. You may find some knees or a hat that you can use for one of your characters. Take notes.

The children you're writing for, however, are far removed from your childhood. Go out and find today's children in their world. Watch what's going on at the park or on a school playground. Watch children and their parents in the grocery store, at the mall, coming out of a movie theater. In a museum cafeteria sit near children on a school trip and listen carefully. Can you tell what's on their minds?

Move closer. Volunteer some time; babysit for a friend; be a teacher's aide once a week; coach a team; lead a scout troop; assist or read aloud at the library. Take notes.

Look for news photographs that include both children and adults. The children may be acting or responding to events differently from the adults in the same situation. Why?

You may have to work hard to see social and cultural forces that are second nature to children. What seems like random running around on a playground takes place within a complex system of territories, hierarchies, and behaviors. Any child can draw for you a map of his or her schoolyard showing home sites for the double-dutch team, the soccer kids, the big girls, the kids who climb, the kids who dig, the kids who stand and watch. Your guide may not be aware of how much he or she knows, but you can bet it's enough to survive recess.

Besides giving you material for stories, getting a sense of children's lives will also remind you of children's restless, inquisitive energy. It will remind you that whether a child must be browbeaten into reading for twenty minutes a day or picks up a book at every chance, he or she has many other things to do. Soccer practice is in an hour; his friend is on the phone; today is her sister's birthday. Be sure this child will be eager to pick up your book again, once it's been thrown down.

Spending time with children may be particularly helpful in writing dialogue and learning about relationships among kids. What do they giggle about when adults aren't around? Just how rude are they? What words do they use when they think they're alone? The more you can get yourself into situations where you're an insignificant presence, the more useful talk you may overhear. Since children in the back seat seem to treat a car's driver as part of the machinery, car-pool duty may yield some useful exchanges. Sit behind children on a bus or at the movies. Take notes.

Be aware of your own childlike experiences. How do you feel the first day in a new class or as part of a group where you know no one, where you don't know what's expected of you? What happens inside you when the authorities at work change the rules? Do you keep a hidden cache of your favorite snack? Ah! You're human, quite like children.

Exercises

Does your central child character behave as a child? Could he or she believably step onto your local playground and feel at home—or feel alien in a childlike way? How close are your character's feelings and thoughts to your own as a child? If you're doubtful about the believability of your central child character, try listing moments and speeches that show his or her childlike qualities. Let those encourage you to do more.

What advice would you give a child who wanted to write the story you mean to write? A jolting thought! Why *would* a child write your story? What about it would appeal to a child? What would a child add, cut out, enlarge? This exercise should help you to think about your story as a child might.

PART THREE

Making Your Story Whole

TWELVE

Your Theme, Yourself

> A work cannot be a success unless one loves its governing idea.
> —Leo Tolstoy, qtd. in Henri Troyat's *Tolstoy*

> People . . . write about violent things because they are angry inside and instead of acting it out they want to write about it.
> —A fourth-/fifth-grade boy

> People like to write about violence because they see violent movies, because they see it on the streets and on TV and they have to talk about it. And if they can't talk about it, they have to get it out some way, so they write about it.
> —Another fourth-/fifth-grade boy

Reviewers often speak of theme. "She explores her theme," from a hundred reviews and essays, always makes me uneasy. At first I thought my discomfort came from a doubt that I, as a writer, was up to all this important exploring. I've slowly learned that my uneasiness is as a reader: I don't read to explore themes. I read, as children read, to see what happens.

Yet theme *is* crucial to a well-told story. The three main posts that support a story—plot, character, and setting—rest on the bedrock of that story's theme. The theme is probably what calls an author to a story. You write because you have to tell about something—something connected to you.

A woman who has spent a lifetime reading and editing children's books told me that the theme is what drives the story. Inspiration grows from a theme, she says, and it is the deep-down understanding the writer wants to leave with the reader.

The theme is often linked to the story's scale. For example, while a story about a boy who enters a sled race for the prize money in order to save his family's farm is exciting, and even complete, it's nevertheless a simple tale of courage and determination. But that the Indian who races against the boy is also trying to save *his* people's land from the government magnifies both the scale and the power of the story. *Stone Fox* resonates with deeper meaning through its theme of the enduring connection of people to their land.

Although concentrating on a story's theme and its permutations may be right and proper for critics, this is usually a destructive way for authors to approach their stories. You'll do better to build your story on a concrete instance rather than on an abstract theme. Let the thematic material come out unconsciously.

Systematically building a novel from a theme can be deadening. When people tell me about their stories by describing their themes—often meant to teach children something—the stories that follow are usually wooden. These writers are so keen on "exploring" that they may even neglect to tell readers what happens next to the characters. Instead, each scene does its tedious job of illustrating an aspect of the theme.

For most writers I've worked with the impetus for a novel comes from something interesting and important to them: a curious character, a scary incident, a funny "what if," a yearning to live vicariously in Elizabethan England. Lloyd Alexander says that the Welsh settings for his Prydain novels intrigued him long before he had his plots or characters. Thus, although the theme may underlie everything, the work begins with having a good story to tell about so-and-so and his or her attempt to do such-and-such in this-or-that time and place.

This underlying presence of theme doesn't mean anything mystical, simply that you are you, and if you write out of yourself your story will reflect you. If you've begun in good faith—because your story is important to you—work on. Be confident that your theme, grounded in your beliefs and concerns, is in your story. You couldn't keep it out.

Part of your work in writing may involve discovering your theme and subthemes. You may discover these interior structures slowly, only after you're a long way into your work. Or you may suddenly understand what your mind, half-knowing, has put on the page. Ask yourself why certain images keep cropping up. Be alert to the patterns and connections; ponder why you've included a scene that appears to be unconnected to the story. Take the time to think through what your story is about at its deepest level.

Once you understand that your story is about longing for family or political courage or the dangers (or glory) of a devil-may-care attitude, you can use the theme as a tool for shaping your work. You can test digressions against it, for instance, as you decide whether or not to keep them.

Since themes and subthemes connect a novel's parts and bind them into a whole, you can work with yours to unify your story. Ideally, as your novel moves toward its climax everything will be connected and will reflect whatever motivated you to write.

This sense of wholeness comes when everything in a story works together. The plot seems to be inseparable from the characters. The characters sit comfortably in the chairs of the setting. The images are appropriate to the time and place—for example, clouds in a caveman story are not like jet-trails but like a mammoth's steaming breath. The narrator seems to feel that the story is worth the telling. The outcome of the characters' struggles, though perhaps surprising, feels inevitable. The story is of a piece.

Whether or not the reader is aware of the theme, the story

will *feel* whole. As naturally as a raccoon is born in a cavity high in the sycamore by the crawfish-bearing stream, so the well-told story seems to be naturally born. But it isn't. As every writer knows, wholeness is the result of hard work.

Exercises

Keep a list of your main theme and subthemes as you discover them. Keep this page handy and work with the themes as your story evolves and you get to know it better. Ponder the list from time to time, particularly when you feel stuck.

Using this list, write summaries of your story that emphasize different themes. Does the story change in any ways that are useful to you? How do the secondary characters echo these themes? Do you want to enlarge or enhance their stories?

THIRTEEN

Finding a Voice

The six voices that follow coax readers to begin their stories. Each is quite different from the others. Try reading them aloud.

In the High and Far-Off Times the Elephant, O Best Beloved, had no trunk. (Rudyard Kipling, "The Elephant's Child")

It's a funny thing about mothers and fathers. Even when their own child is the most disgusting little blister you could ever imagine, they still think that he or she is wonderful. (Roald Dahl, *Matilda*)

The day Shiloh come, we're having us a big Sunday dinner. Dara Lynn's dipping bread in her glass of cold tea, the way she likes, and Becky pushes her beans up over the edge of her plate in her rush to get 'em down. (Phyllis Reynolds Naylor, *Shiloh*)

We moved on the Tuesday before Labor Day. I knew what the weather was like the second I got up. I knew because I caught my mother sniffing under her arms. She always does that when it's hot and humid, to make sure her deodorant's working. I don't use deodorant yet. I don't think people start to smell bad until they're at least twelve. So I've still got a few months to go. (Judy Blume, *Are You There God? It's Me, Margaret*)

In the land of Ingary, where such things as seven-league boots and cloaks of invisibility really exist, it is quite a misfortune to be born the eldest of three. Everyone knows you are the one who will fail first, and worst, if the three of you set out to seek your fortunes.

Sophie Hatter was the eldest of three sisters. She was not even the child of a poor woodcutter, which might have given her some chance of success. (Diana Wynne Jones, *Howl's Moving Castle*)

"Tom!"
No answer.
"Tom!"
No answer.
"What's gone with that boy, I wonder? You, TOM!"
No answer.
The old lady pulled her spectacles down and looked over them, about the room; then she put them up and looked out under them. She seldom or never looked *through* them for so small a thing as a boy. (Mark Twain, *The Adventures of Tom Sawyer*)

If theme is the bedrock of fiction and plot, character, and setting are its three structural posts, then the voice that tells the story is the wrapping in which it is presented to the reader. This wrapping, however, cannot be removed or separated from its underlying structure.

The voice is an integral part of a novel, binding it into a whole. Just so, the French horn playing a Mozart horn concerto does much more than deliver a certain pattern of notes to the listener's ear. The horn's voice contributes qualities—humor, richness, power—that belong with this melody and help connect the listener to it emotionally. A change in instrument—say, the same note pattern transcribed for bassoon or harpsichord—might be unsettling, might feel completely wrong. A story told in a different voice becomes a different story.

A novel's voice is related to, but different from, its point of view, which means from what or whose perspective the story is told (see chapter 18). An appropriate voice, whether it's recounting the adventures of Huck Finn or Mary Poppins, adds an aura of truth to a story. The voice you use can be plain or highly characterized, as long as it conveys your sense of the story.

As in any human communication, your novel's tone of voice must suggest and define for your readers their relationship to what you say. A scene showing a child on a runaway donkey could be funny, exciting, scary, or heartbreaking. How readers respond, how they enter your story, depends on character and context but also on the narrative voice.

Imagine the tale of an orphan child abandoned to live alone, undisciplined, making a mess of her home, disruptive at school. Another morose modern problem novel? Not when it's presented in the voice that Astrid Lindgren uses to tell us *Pippi Longstocking.*

At the start, the voice must woo the reader, gaining his or her trust, making the reader comfortable as he or she enters the novel, hinting at glories to come, transmitting a sense of the story's importance, and demonstrating that you, the author, are in control. The voice says, "This happened!" or, at the least, "Let's pretend this happened—we'll have a great time!"

From then on the voice you've chosen must carry out your first responsibility: to make the story clear. It must sustain the reader's belief and help him or her comprehend the story's structure and coherence, all the while adding to the novel's richness and the reader's pleasure.

A voice that is intrusive, manipulative, dry, self-important, or just too cute can damage your story. You must be certain that a chuckle on the side, the underscoring of some lesson, or even a single false word doesn't undercut your story by getting in the way of the reader's absorption.

Most stories are probably best presented to the reader in a discreet, straightforward manner, skipping the flourishes and the difficulties of sustaining, consistently and pleasurably, a highly stylized voice. If you're a beginning author, and unless you're certain that a particular voice is right for your story, you would do well to choose a voice that efficiently and enjoyably gives the reader the facts.

A voice expressing a highly charged attitude toward the events can add a great deal to a story if it's well developed. One of Roald Dahl's strengths was his amusing, opinionated, emphatic tone: This is what happened—and this is how to think about it! Isn't it an outrage? Isn't it fabulous? Or even—given Dahl's seductive, slippery, us-versus-them moral relativism—isn't it both? In just a few pages of *Fantastic Mr. Fox* Dahl moves the reader from high indignation on behalf of his cheated hero to high glee as his hero turns around and cheats someone else.

The voice in your story must be used consistently throughout. No one wants to read a novel that starts in a rich comic voice and then subsides into a bland, pedestrian one—perhaps an indication that the author's energy flagged—only to charge forward at the climax in a voice overloaded with energetic adjectives. The reader, if he or she is still reading, will be confused and possibly annoyed.

Even Mark Twain could be inconsistent. He began to write *The Adventures of Tom Sawyer* as a memory of his boyhood, and occasionally lapses from the rich, immediate sense of This Happened into a distancing, sentimental chuckle about How Boys

Are. Child readers want the voice to tell them the story, not tell them *about* the story.

In many contemporary first-person novels, the narrator will insert a comment or a wisecrack at the end of just about every paragraph. This makes for choppy writing—and reading—as the flow of the story halts so the one-liners can be delivered. I discovered a bad case of stop-and-go writing in one of my own manuscripts, and after I lopped the last sentences off many paragraphs, the character's developing story flowed more smoothly, though it wasn't quite so "clever." I've wished the author had done the same in many a novel I've read since.

The value of the right voice can't be overestimated. Stories that are in trouble can be transformed by a change in voice. From forced and overcontrolled, they become natural, believable, engrossing.

The success of J. K. Rowling's Harry Potter books rests in large part on their voice. Readers connect with that long before they meet Harry, and throughout the novels the voice remains central to their pleasure. Rowling is marvelously inventive, and her novels' confident, funny voice, taking magic as a given, helps readers draw something from just about every part of the story. Readers don't notice that a scene is tangential to the plot or when the hero is barely there. The mysteries and dangers of Harry's predicaments arise from time to time; the cheerful voice permeates the story.

My niece, who loves the Potter books and has read each one several times, has put them in their place, which is here and there around her house. Wherever she is she can pick one up, open it at random, and plunge in. She doesn't care where she finds herself in which story because she loves reading anything about Hogwarts and Harry, any place and any time.

You may have noticed that I haven't said much about how to find the right voice for your story. It's hard to be helpful about this. There's no formula, for each novel's voice will be, should be, unique. Sometimes a voice just comes, but often you'll have to work to find it. Study other authors' work. Read aloud one of your scenes written in various voices you think you might use. Think of how much your narrator knows and cares as part of the drama. Read about dialogue in chapter 19. These steps all might help. Chances are that if you keep working you'll feel your way to a voice that sounds true.

The right voice is confident, trustworthy, perhaps entertaining, and completely at one with the story it tells. The right voice conveys belief in the story and belief that it's worth telling. More than any other aspect of writing, the right voice induces readers to give themselves over to a story.

Exercise

Try writing your first few paragraphs in several different voices, as if to prepare readers for different experiences: give a comic touch to events, a mysterious cast, a foreboding of tragedy. How would the tone change if you used as your opening Snoopy's signature phrase, "It was a dark and stormy night"? Madeleine L'Engle used this to begin *A Wrinkle in Time* and a fine story followed.

What you want is the voice that most effectively conveys your story, a voice you can control and sustain. One tone of voice will feel right, though you may want to shift it a little, this way or that, a little more closely involved, a little more distant, in certain scenes.

FOURTEEN

Many Ways to Tell the Same Story

> [T]he folk fairy tale . . . is the result of a story being shaped and
> reshaped by being told millions of times, by different adults to
> all kinds of other adults and children. Each narrator, as he told
> the story, dropped and added elements to make it more mean-
> ingful to himself and to the listeners, whom he knew well.
> When talking to a child, the adult responded to what he sur-
> mised from the child's reactions.
>
> —Bruno Bettelheim, *The Uses of Enchantment*

My young daughter and I sat on the couch as I told about Gold-
ilocks and the three bears. "And the wee little baby bear climbed
into his chair and began to eat his porridge," I said. "Her," said
an authoritative voice from beside me. "Her" it was, from then on.

Anyone who tells a story to a child finds his or her own way
to tell it. Bruno Bettelheim recommends that parents tell, rather than read, fairy stories to their children. In telling, he suggests,
parents will naturally stress, enlarge, embroider, and go more
deeply into the parts of the story that most interest their child.
The teller finds, consciously or unconsciously, the story his or her
listeners need to hear—and also, perhaps, the one the teller needs
to tell.

A printed story, of course, will not adjust itself to each reader. But as your story is being written and is still malleable, you
will choose, over and over, to tell it this way or that. Just as a jury
must consider whether different stories, whole and consistent, can
be woven from the same set of "facts," so each of your choices
will result in a different playing out of the material. Often you'll
make your choices unconsciously—but to help remind you that

you *are* choosing, here are some instances of variations on a single story or event.

An instance: The science teacher in an elementary school where I was working arranged to have a friend's son bring in his pet boa constrictor. I urged the other teachers to have their students write about the visit. The big day came. The high school student held court, draped with a creature I remember as being twelve feet long and as thick as a car tire. The children were brought in class by class. Here are two different versions of what they saw.

An excited kindergarten boy found just the word he needed next to the letter S on an illustrated alphabet banner running high around his classroom. He ran back and forth between the wall and his desk, harvesting—remembering—the letters one by one. His report on the visit was, in its entirety: "S N A K E."

A sixth-grade girl began her story, "A young man brought his boa constrictor to school today, and we all went to see it in the science room. He had light brown skin and curly black hair." A hairy snake? A failure of scientific observation? Totally confused, I went on to read her description of the visitor who was, to her, by far the more interesting.

Another instance, one you may know: When a children's book is illustrated, the artist (who is usually not the author) joins in telling the story, often rendering not the author's vision of the story but his or her own. Imagine Roald Dahl's *Matilda* without illustrations, just the author's angry prose. Now think of Quentin Blake's delicate drawings showing Matilda and Miss Honey as pure goodness. The effect is of two simultaneous tellings, each with its own emphasis within the same story—and a book children love.

It's clear that people may see or understand the same facts differently or, as with children's books, may hear or see or draw or tell or write the same story differently. One way you choose to tell your story probably seems to *be* the story. But the choices—tale, chapter book, or novel; first- or third-person narrator; girl, boy, adult, or animal main character; long ago or present-day setting; a voice that is involved or distant, sweet or furious—can be made thoughtfully as well as intuitively. As you plan and write, even as you revise (and especially when something isn't working), be aware that other possibilities may better suit, better contain and present your story.

Exercise

Tell your story briefly to a child you know well. Your story, long nurtured in the dim, rich hothouse of your secret hopes, is suddenly brought out into stark, bright sunlight. You see it as it really is—for that one child. Did you make major changes as you told it to please or interest this particular listener? Would these changes make the written version better?

You may decide to try telling your story another way. You may decide to try another child.

INTERLUDE: A PIG'S TALE

Do you recognize this story?

A newborn pig is taken from his family to a farm where he'll be fattened for eating. He and the other animals on the farm can talk to each other, though not to humans. The pig is dear and innocent; he doesn't know he'll be killed. He makes good friends among the other animals, and one, a mother figure who is patient, strong, and far more worldly than he is, comforts and teaches him. With her help the pig avoids being butchered and wins an award in a local farm contest before a cheering crowd.

Isn't *that* a story! Or two? *Charlotte's Web* by E. B. White, published in 1952? Or *Babe the Gallant Pig* by Dick King-Smith, published in 1983? Do we really need *two* stories about a tender piglet saved from slaughter with the help of a friend?

The answer to all of these questions is absolutely "Yes!" We need the utterly different and wonderful stories of Wilbur and Babe.

However much one plot may resemble another, different authors will tell the story in their own way, with their own feelings, their own voice, their own theme. The same story, for instance, may be presented in a straightforward manner, clearly and traditionally formed (as *Babe* is), or layered with many meanings (as *Charlotte's Web* is).

Usually children's novels follow a direct and uncomplicated narrative line. Where they don't, they can be a mess—or they can be magical. *Babe* is well told, imaginative, comic, heart-thumping, deeply satisfying. *Charlotte's Web* is all of that and it's also more complex, its disparate parts connected by White's rich understanding of human and animal nature.

The difference between *Charlotte's Web* and *Babe* is, in part, their themes. In Peter F. Neumeyer's *Annotated Charlotte's Web,* White says his novel is "essentially . . . a hymn to the barn," "a story of friendship, life, death, salvation," "a story of miracles." *Charlotte's Web* holds out the comforting thought that when you're in terrible danger and don't know what to do, a strong friend will come along to save you.

In *Something about the Author: Facts and Pictures about Authors and Illustrators* (ed. Anne Commire, 1987), King-Smith says, "If there is a philosophical point behind what I write, I'm not especially conscious of it. Maybe I do stress the need for courage, something we all wish we had more of, and I also do feel strongly for underdogs." *Babe* offers the hope that when you're in terrible danger you'll find a friend to help you do what you must to prevail. In his unflagging effort to become a sheep-herding pig, Babe shows that we need not accept the limitations others presume for us. When his work saves him from death, we feel that a pure heart, persevering courageously, can overcome adversity. Also, it never hurts to be polite.

Although I admire *Charlotte's Web,* which many people consider a masterpiece, *Babe* affects me more strongly. I think the key is in the titles. The gallant Babe works hard to help himself; his innocence is active and valiant. By contrast, Wilbur doesn't do much for himself; he's tearful, fearful, passive, and feels sorry for himself. Most of all, he waits for Charlotte to save him. He may seem charmingly familiar to young readers, but he's too much of a wimp for me.

There's also a difference in voice. King-Smith's tale, with its clear, direct prose, isn't interpreted but hits the reader full force. The narrator takes Babe's struggle with utter seriousness. White's voice, often more distant, though always charming, lapses from time to time into philosophical commentary, breaking my enchantment when he suggests what I should think.

These two different voices each support their stories in ways that are appropriate to the authors' themes. They each present very different pig tales.

PART FOUR

The Reader as Storyteller

FIFTEEN

Show, Don't Tell

Show, don't tell.

—Every writing teacher, ever

Beginning writers have lots of questions about showing rather than telling: What does it mean? Why should you do it? When should you do it? How do you do it?

"Show, don't tell" means that instead of telling readers that something happened, you show them the scene so that they *see* it happening. Showing gives readers the satisfying illusion that there's no intermediary between them and the characters. More subtly, instead of being told the meaning of a situation or event, readers are given the opportunity to take in the meaning directly. Watching something happen is almost always more vivid and thus more interesting than being told about it.

There's nothing wrong with telling. Events that occur between scenes may usefully be compressed into a narrative. A scene may go on for so long the reader longs for the relief of an expeditious summary. But when you come to an event that's too important or rich or amusing to short-circuit with a summary, it's time to let your readers *hear* the voices and *see* the action. As a TV announcer might say, "Now we go to the characters. Live!"

The process of story writing is selective. As the author, you'll choose when to compress a story ("Once upon a time in a kingdom by the sea there was a king who had three beautiful daughters") and when to provide a full-blown scene using both narration and dialogue ("One day the king summoned the youngest princess to the throne room and said, 'The time has come for you to choose a husband.' He struck his scepter three times against a map of the neighboring kingdoms: 'There! There! Or there!'").

You'll also choose, almost without being aware of it, not to tell or show almost everything that happens to your characters throughout the time covered by the story. Readers don't have to know what the princess ate for breakfast that fateful morning or that her allergies were acting up.

Although I'm an advocate of using summaries as a writing tool, don't let working with them encourage you to rely too much on telling and too little on showing. Characters who are controlled too tightly, who are marched through appointed events toward a given climax, may seem wooden when compared with those who are allowed to speak and breathe and move around in scenes.

This danger of using summaries was mentioned to me by Betsy Hearne, the author of *Choosing Books for Children*. After reading an earlier version of my manuscript she commented that "many beginning writers depend too much on describing events from the outside rather than developing them from the inside— i.e., on summarizing (telling) rather than showing." She suggested that beginners might profit from examples of writers who don't use summaries but work in other ways. (Her comment was gratefully taken, and a revised and expanded chapter 6 is the result. This is a nice example of a wise, alert reader helping one writer improve her manuscript.)

In the first chapters of *The Secret Garden*, Frances Hodgson Burnett uses a sustained intertwining of showing and telling to set up a tension that draws readers in and carries them along for many pages. She announces at the outset, "When Mary Lennox was sent to Misselthwaite Manor to live with her uncle everybody said she was the most disagreeable-looking child ever seen. It was true, too." Readers are *told* exactly what to think of Mary.

Burnett continues to show as well as tell her readers more about the nastiness of her heroine. Yet she intersperses small scenes that *show* a different Mary and encourage readers to suspect that Mary has a more interesting side. For example, one morning, while she was still living in India, Mary woke up and heard a rustling. "[W]hen she looked down she saw a little snake gliding along and watching her with eyes like jewels. She was not frightened, because he was a harmless little thing who would not hurt her and he seemed in a hurry to get out of the room. He slipped under the door as she watched him."

That's the entire scene. Readers see that this disagreeable girl is knowledgeable about snakes and fearless when she finds one in her bedroom. By the end of the second chapter, although Mary is no less unpleasant, readers have seen for themselves that she's brave, smart, empathetic to those in trouble, curious, and eager to make gardens wherever she goes. They've discovered, perhaps unconsciously, that she's a complex, interesting person about whom they may be curious to learn more.

When should you switch from telling to showing? Follow your instincts but also consider the following: Has the narration gone on so long that readers will welcome the variety of on-the-scene action? Is a scene just too good—too comic, too frightening, too rich with character—*not* to show it rather than just tell about it? Most important, is the event crucial to the story, thus needing the emphasis of its own scene?

Mark Twain had a good sense of what readers would enjoy. How unsatisfying it would be to have only a distant telling of the moment when Tom, Huck, and Joe hide in the church balcony and witness their own funeral. Instead, Twain puts his readers downstairs in the pews to enjoy the resurrection—and they're almost as surprised as Aunt Polly when the three march down the aisle.

By contrast, how tedious it would be to spend every slow hour with Huck and Jim on the raft. Instead, Twain summarizes their river journey—dawn and twilight, current and sandbar, ship and shore light. When he does put in a scene, it usually gives us a taste of the trip and also furthers the plot or moves along the developing relationship between Huck and Jim. With a combination of compression and scene, Twain skillfully brings us through his stories.

Mildred D. Taylor wrote a remarkable scene in *Roll of Thunder, Hear My Cry* wherein "Show, don't tell" is invoked by one of the characters for the same reasons an author would. Cassie Logan's mother is distressed to learn that, despite being told over and over not to, her children have gone to the Wallace store—a place that is unsafe for blacks. "Although she scolded us severely, she did not whip us. We were sent to bed early but we didn't consider that a punishment, and we doubted that Mama did either. How we managed to escape a whipping we couldn't fathom until Saturday, when Mama woke us before dawn and piled us into the wagon."

Mama drives the children to the home of Mr. and Mrs. Berry. Mrs. Berry greets them warmly, but Mr. Berry is little more than a presence in a dark corner. "A still form lay there staring at us with glittering eyes. The face had no nose, and the head no hair; the skin was scarred, burned, and the lips were wizened black, like charcoal. As the wheezing sound echoed from the opening that was a mouth, Mama said, 'Say good morning to Mrs. Berry's husband, children.'"

The family stays for an hour's visit. "After we were on the main road again, having ridden in thoughtful silence over the wooded trail, Mama said quietly, 'The Wallaces did that, children. They poured kerosene over Mr. Berry and his nephews and lit them afire. . . . They're bad people, the Wallaces. That's why I don't want you to ever go to their store again—for any reason. You understand?'"

Telling her children hadn't worked, so Mama shows them why they must never go to the Wallace store. Readers also understand and are left with a greater respect for the Logan household's many rules.

The play and interplay of condensed telling and more expansive showing is useful for controlling the pace of a story. You may want to use an outline or summary to pinpoint the important events so that you can consider whether each should be emphasized with a scene.

Exercises

If you're reading a novel now, make it a point to be aware of when the author switches from telling to showing and back again. Try to understand why and how the switch occurs.

Do the same as you reread a draft chapter of your own novel. Find a place where you've used a compressed version of events that might make a good scene and write the scene. Try to squeeze every possible bit of drama or humor from the incident.

Even if, in the end, you decide that telling works better than showing in this instance, writing the scene may give you material—perhaps just one perfect word—that will make the narrative richer, livelier, more complex, more interesting, true.

SIXTEEN

Filling in the Gaps

> The character that is rendered too meticulously often fails to convince. Too little is left for the reader to contribute out of himself. General physical descriptions are usually enough; the reader will supply his own visual image and because it is his own it will be a reality for him.
>
> —William Sloane, *The Craft of Writing*

Keep your reader—like your main character—in an active mode. Instead of passively receiving the story, the reader, through being present at scenes and figuring out what's going on, will absorb the story as a new part of his or her experience.

All of us call on our imaginations to fill in gaps in what we know. If, on a downtown sidewalk, we see an otherwise well-dressed man wearing one dress shoe and one sneaker, we tell ourselves a quick story to explain his situation. One person's explanation may be sympathetic, another's mocking. In a novel, curious and unexplained characters or events also evoke readers' conscious or unconscious attempts to understand.

Anyone who has discussed a book or movie with others has seen how differently people react to stories. A reader enters a story in subtle ways, making assumptions and guesses about all kinds of things based on his or her own experiences and knowledge of the world. By filling in gaps in their own way, readers find their own meanings in scenes and in the story and become more actively engaged in it—and thus bound more closely to it.

I once saw a literal filling in of gaps in a copy of Picasso's *Family of Saltimbanques* (reproduced on page 37). This *Saltimbanques,* about two feet square, was resting on a window sill in a day shelter for homeless women. One of the women had found the reproduction and was reworking it. She came to the shelter every few days "to work on my Picasso."

Picasso had left many open spaces surrounding, behind, and between his figures, possibly to express a feeling of emptiness and isolation. The homeless painter had changed that. In her version, the original design and people remained, but she made the distant sands less bleak by adding a sea with gulls flying above. In the middle ground she painted three sheltering trees. In the foreground a patch of grass now curled around the feet of the stern man on the left, spread across the bottom, supporting the little girl, and continued to the right border and up, enclosing the once-isolated woman with the others. This painter had "read" Picasso's mysterious painting and made of it the story she wanted it to be. She gave shelter to the travelers and connected the woman to the man and child, making this work her own.

Just so, leaving gaps can result in a richer story for individual readers who create their own understandings about what is not told. How do writers do this? Begin at the simplest level, by leaving transitions from one scene to another partly up to the reader.

In *The Adventures of Tom Sawyer,* Mark Twain leaves a gap in time and space before the scene in which Tom and his friends appear at their own funeral. When last we saw them, the boys were on the island, smoking away. We know they know about the funeral plans; we don't know what they'll do next. The next chapter begins in town and stays with the mournful townfolks right through the funeral. When the boys appear, any reader who wishes to can imagine how they rowed ashore before sunrise, stealthily worked their way through the streets to the church, and waited in the gallery through the solemn service before springing their surprise. There was no need for Twain to slow the story at that point to tell readers exactly how they got there.

Once your story is well begun, you can take shortcuts through routine events. A smart writer once told me to treat scenes like parties: come late, leave early. This lets the reader enjoy the meat of the story without having to watch every fork and knife being laid in preparation or every dish being washed and put away. The involved reader can fill in the sense of all this.

Entering a scene in progress helps to draw the reader into the story. He or she isn't left hanging around an empty, though beautifully described, room waiting for someone to come in. Some scenes in Judy Blume's fast-moving *Superfudge,* for example, last only a few paragraphs, with no time wasted getting in or out.

If you do leave some aspects of your story for readers to figure out, be careful to keep things clear. Be sure the clues from which they can build an understanding about what's going on are honest and helpful, rather than teases that jolt or delay the story's flow and may frustrate and overwhelm their interest.

Although you can encourage your readers to participate in telling your story, you can't control how they do it. Just as you must find your way to tell the story, each reader must find his or her own way to read it. You have no idea of the different versions of your published story that will be spun in readers' minds. A woman who had been a public health worker once told me that a novel of mine, which has some minor parent/child skirmishes over what was for supper, was a story about nutrition. That certainly hadn't been my intent, but that's what my story was for her.

Can we ask children, who have limited experiences on which to build, to enter into the making of our stories? Absolutely! Much of what children know of the world comes from their continuing work filling in gaps and silences, from guessing and intuiting what adults mean or have done or are likely to do. Harriet, of Louise Fitzhugh's *Harriet the Spy,* is just one of hundreds of heroes and heroines—and millions of children—who figures out what she needs to know based on her own observations. With a clear hint or two, readers will be ready and eager to do the same with your story.

Exercise

Find a scene in your story that you sense goes on too long. Try entering it later and leaving earlier. Do you like the results? Will readers get all they need—factually and for pleasure—from the shorter scene? Will they be able to fill in any gaps you've left in the narrative?

You may find this exercise worth trying with every scene. It will focus your mind on what the scene is really about and why it's of value in your story. If you get carried away, though, you may find yourself with a novel that is too succinct and shorter than is effective.

INTERLUDE: DIDACTICISM VERSUS VICARIOUS EXPERIENCE

[*Warning:* This is a boring quotation. Please read it.]

"Frank's Campaign" is the record of a boy's experiences, by whom the cares and responsibilities of manhood are voluntarily assumed, and nobly and successfully borne. He supplies his father's place while the latter is absent in his country's service, and is enabled, by a fortunate circumstance, to pay off the mortgage resting on the home farm.

Nothing is claimed for the young hero which may not be achieved by an energetic and manly boy of the same age. It is hoped that the record of Frank's struggles and final success may stimulate the boys who may read it to manly endeavor, and to a faithful and conscientious discharge of whatever duties may devolve upon them.

—Horatio Alger, *Frank's Campaign*

The spirit of Horatio Alger lives on in the hopes of many who want to write for children or who purposefully put novels in children's hands. An educator once told me that children's novels are books "in which children are required to grow in a situation." I gritted my teeth. How could this admirable woman have gotten it so wrong? I don't "require" anything of my characters—or my readers. I try to invite readers in and hope they enjoy the story.

Perhaps it's inevitable that people write for children in part from a desire to teach, to mine their own experiences and accumulated wisdom for the benefit of the next generation. Although this impulse can never be entirely suppressed, those who write for kids must be alert to it so they can control the impulse rather than overcontrol, and possibly ruin, their stories.

It's all too easy for writers to imagine a teacher or parent reading their golden words to children who sit there absorbing and benefiting from them all. It's harder to remember that publishing a novel is not a license to instruct others or an opportunity to make over the world—even if you happen to know exactly how to fix everything that's gone wrong.

There are two good reasons not to preach to young readers. Most important is that message-driven stories—like their close relation, stories that are consciously theme-driven—are often dull. Children may sense when a tedious lesson is bearing down on them and simply shut your book.

Because didactic stories are often full of telling rather than showing, a writer who wants to educate minds may find it hard to make the story live. Take a look at Mark Twain's *The Prince and the Pauper* and *A Connecticut Yankee in King Arthur's Court*. These novels are appreciated for their intriguing central situations and some good scenes, but in each the actual chapter-by-chapter stories get bogged down in political haranguing.

The deadliness of most preachy tales may be why some of

the best-told stories grow out of parents' entertainment for their own children. Any storyteller who has experienced the fidgeting, the "When's supper?," the child slowly standing, gazing about, wandering off, has learned when to throw in a zinger or cut to the chase. Retold stories usually have had any didactic flaws worn away.

If you write to teach your readers something, you're likely to manipulate your characters to fit the message. But children have keen antennae for the ways of the powerful and the plight of the powerless. They'll sense when you're jerking your characters around to make a point—and jerking your readers around as well.

Even if children would hold still for it, there's a second reason to avoid preaching: it probably won't work. Just as it's human nature to tell others what to do, it's human nature not to listen. Children like to find out for themselves.

Children are also more likely to learn from experience than from what they're told. If a cautionary tale is helpful at all it's probably helpful *after* the fact, providing language with which to assess and name an important experience, to lock in its meaning. Although you read a book like this one eager to be taught, it's through your active experience of writing that you'll really learn. Doing the suggested exercises is more valuable than reading about them.

However, a reader can learn from the kind of vicarious experiences the engaged reading of fiction provides. When a child is "present" at a story's events, absorbing as if personally what happens to the hero, working to fill in gaps in understanding, in a sense that child experiences those events directly. So tell the best story you can. Show the truth about what the characters do. Then, as your reader enters into a conspiracy with you to get the characters through their trials, he or she will have the vicarious sense of making choices, taking action, reaping the consequences. Your reader may, as from real experience, *learn.*

Sometimes even authors who are careful not to shove a message at their readers can't resist summing things up all too clearly at the end. They bring in a wise elder or create a super event to blast their point home, often boring or confusing their readers. Although novels often do have a moment, even a conversation, that expresses the meaning of the story, it's best if this works *in* character, *within* the plot, a natural part of the story. The meaning, like the climax, grows out of what has happened before. Writing a preachy set piece is as out of place as flying by in a plane writing your message huge on blue sky.

A strongly felt, well-written novel is shaped by the author's sensibility and communicates his or her deepest beliefs. If you write a good story, the teaching will take care of itself.

To borrow a few words from Horatio Alger, remember that the "cares and responsibilities" of children's authors are "voluntarily assumed" and their "duty" not to preach must be "borne" and "discharged" "faithfully" and "conscientiously," even "nobly." (How does it feel to be on the receiving end?)

Exercise

Write a summing-up speech for a wise teacher figure in your novel, laying out your message directly for a child reader. Or write a paragraph in which your main character muses about the lessons learned from the experiences you've put him or her through.

There. You've had the satisfaction of writing exactly what you think. Now put those pages aside and let your readers enjoy your story.

A Note to the Reader

In *Aspects of the Novel,* E. M. Forster writes, "Nearly all novels are feeble at the end. . . . If it was not for death and marriage I do not know how the average novelist would conclude."

Since this book is not a novel, I can hardly send it surging pell-mell toward a satisfying death or marriage. In any case, the conclusion is largely up to you. The choices and actions are yours. What the consequences of working on your novel will be—publication and thousands of readers?—none of us can know.

What I can do is point out that from here on the chapters cover a miscellany of nitty-gritty stylistic and technical concerns. You may wish to take a break for now, get on with your writing, then come back to these chapters and exercises, or return to others, for practical advice when a particular issue or problem arises.

PART FIVE

Nitty-Gritty Matters

SEVENTEEN

What Makes a Good Beginning?

Ma, don't you love books that go right into the story without blabbing about who everybody was and everything?

—My daughter, age 10

Whether by "beginning" you mean the first sentence, the first paragraph, or the first chapter, it's that blabbing you want to avoid. If instead you seem to say, "Have I got a story for you! Come on in," chances are readers will happily accept your invitation.

Your first chapter should provide the groundwork for everything that follows. How do you signal to readers what the story is about, get them to trust your way of telling it, give them the facts they must know *plus* get your story off to an enticing start?

There's so much to cover at first that you risk smothering your readers' interest in an avalanche of information. Reading the first pages of a number of novels will show you how some writers have gotten their readers interested—or failed to do so. Look again at the book beginnings quoted at the head of chapter 13. Which books would you choose to read?

A straightforward beginning that acknowledges this is a story and quickly and efficiently gets the basics out of the way is one approach. For example, Mary Norton begins *Bed-Knob and Broomstick:*

> Once upon a time there were three children, and their names were Carey, Charles, and Paul. Carey was about your age, Charles a little younger, and Paul was only six.

> One summer, they were sent to Bedfordshire to stay with an aunt.
> She was an old aunt and lived in an old square house.

Perfect. It's summertime and there are no parents (and barely any aunt) to get in the way of a lovely country adventure. Best of all, the reader is included.

"Who, what, when, why, and where"—the mantra of English teachers and newspaper editors—applies here. Readers will soon become uneasy if they don't learn some particulars. They'll be wary of giving themselves over to your story until they're confident that you'll tell—or show—them what they need to know.

Be sure that the sex of the central character is clear, as well as his or her age or grade in school. Each child reader has an age, a grade, and a sex and may have strong feelings about them.

Plant your characters' feet firmly on a specific piece of ground. Your story happens someplace, sometime. Let readers know, early, where and when.

Take care with the tone of voice you use to begin your story. The voice will suggest and guide your readers' first responses.

If some larger, societal problem parallels, contains, or complicates the main character's story, it's a good idea to hint at that from the start. You're laying the foundation for that situation as well.

Your readers don't need all the background information at first, though, just enough to allow a satisfying plunge into the action. (For example, see the first paragraphs of Jean Craighead George's *Julie of the Wolves.*) Once readers are hooked on the story, you can slip in the rest of the background in half sentences here and there or cover it in a few paragraphs.

Whatever you tell at the beginning, while the reader is searching for clues, will have added weight. Don't waste space on trivia or give misleading hints or suggest the wrong emphasis. Start the story right away, bringing your readers in at the point where things are about to change. However interesting your central character is, however lively and curious your setting, if there's no need to act, no sense of danger or vindication or treasure to come, there's no story. If matters are stable, there is no story. But give your reader the sense that something's happening and he or she will think it's worthwhile to stick around to find out what.

A writer's job is to make things unstable, fast. Let the reader sense that the hero wants or needs something. A good way is to start with a strong, interesting scene starring your central character—a scene that leaves something unresolved.

Most of the quotes in chapter 13—from the start of their stories—touch on the central conflict or action, even the ending, of the novels. You may find it interesting to reread the first page of any novel as soon as you've finished the last page. You'll likely discover more depth there than you were aware of on your first reading. It's best to work at making your novel whole from the start.

A strong beginning doesn't have to be large in scale. The first chapter of Sydney Taylor's *All-of-a-Kind Family* centers on a lost library book. Taylor begins with a small matter, yet through it the reader meets the five girls in the family and learns about the tensions and affections among them and the habits of the household. Furthermore, though readers don't know it yet, the new "library lady," who is kindness itself, turns out to be crucial to the story.

You can avoid separate, set descriptions of place and character by letting readers mine information from the ongoing story. Here's how Katherine Paterson opens *Bridge to Terabithia*: "*Ba-room, ba-room, ba-room, baripity, baripity, baripity, baripity*— Good. His dad had the pickup going. He could get up now. Jess slid out of bed and into his overalls. He didn't worry about a shirt because once he began running he would be hot as popping grease even if the morning air was chill, or shoes because the bottoms of his feet were by now as tough as his worn-out sneakers." From this brief paragraph readers learn something about Jess, his family, and his surroundings—and the story is underway.

As he or she starts a novel, the reader must get to know not only the central character but the authority on the character's story: you. As the author you're in a delicate position: you know something—the entire story!—that the reader does not. As you begin to tell it, you must earn the reader's trust. In the opening sequences readers learn whether you'll reward their curiosity, use words honestly, and deliver on your hints that something terrific is going to happen. If readers sense that you're confidently in control of the story, you'll gain their confidence. They'll read carefully, eagerly, knowing that your words are worth taking seriously.

Some authors like to start a novel by being mysteriously indirect, using a pronoun ("She . . .") or a description ("the kid in the blue cap") instead of a character's name, or by hinting at an other-worldly setting. That can be enticing—provided your readers don't have to turn too many pages with questions buzzing in their minds like static, preventing the clear transmission of your story. You don't want them warily withholding a portion of their attention until they learn the main character's name. If you choose to be mysterious, the payoff had better be good.

Beware the temptation to tantalize or manipulate your readers. Children aren't as pleased about being teased by a stranger as some adults imagine—it gives them an unpleasant feeling of helplessness. If you're too busy being cute to start off your story effectively, or if you don't explain promptly what readers need to know, or if you're sloppily inconsistent, or if you preach, your readers will soon realize that you're abusing your authorial power. Remember that it's the reader who has the ultimate power: to shut your book.

Many of these guidelines are equally relevant to orienting readers at the start of new sections or chapters—in fact, anywhere you make a transition from one scene to another. Once you've let them know who's present, where, and when, they'll be at ease and can sink back into the story. A simple hint may be all they need to fill in the gaps.

Exercises

Skim through some novels you enjoy and look at how the authors set up for business in the first few paragraphs of each chapter. In *A Girl Named Disaster,* for example, Nancy Farmer begins chapter after chapter with her heroine starting the day in or near the boat in which she has set off to find her father. Similar situations, yet Farmer makes them clear and fresh each time.

Make a short list of all the things your readers must know to understand and enjoy your first scene. When you're done, make the list shorter.

Try writing your first scene simply as an engaging story that comes later in the novel, so that readers already know the necessary background. When you have it well written, slip in any introductory information they require in a few words without interrupting the narrative flow.

INTERLUDE: THE FIRST PARAGRAPH OF *CHARLOTTE'S WEB*

> From the evidence, I had as much trouble getting off the ground [with *Charlotte's Web*] as did the Wright Brothers.
>
> —E. B. White, qtd. in Peter F. Neumeyer's *Annotated Charlotte's Web*

Although E. B. White is the coauthor of one of the classic texts on writing, *The Elements of Style,* he has not been immune to writers' problems. Peter F. Neumeyer's valuable *Annotated Charlotte's Web* allows us to examine how White worked.

White's first draft began, "Charlotte was a big grey spider who lived in a doorway. But there is no use talking about Charlotte until we have talked about her best friend—a pig named Wilbur."

His second draft opened with, "A barn can have a horse in it, and a barn can have a cow in it, and a barn can have hens scratching in the chaff . . . but if a barn hasn't got a pig in it, it is hardly worth talking about."

After another try at starting with the barn, White changed his focus: "I shall speak first of Wilbur." White does speak briefly of Wilbur and then says, as if trying to write himself out of his quandary, "But there is no use talking about Wilbur until we have looked into the matter of the barn."

Later, perhaps feeling that he should start with a scene instead of talking to his readers, White tried writing an introduction, which began: "At midnight, John Arable pulled his boots on, lit a lantern, and walked out through the woods to the hog house."

On his eighth try, White arrived at the opening he would use: "'Where's Papa going with that ax?' said Fern to her mother as they were setting the table for breakfast." Notice how effortlessly we learn who, when, and where—all the while keeping our attention on the all-important what.

White had tried to begin by describing his characters; then he tried to begin by describing his setting. Neither approach worked for the story he wanted to tell. So he switched to an emphasis on the plot: Fern will race out and stop her father from killing the runt of the new pig litter. Most wonderful, this opening not only starts off the plot of saving Wilbur's life but also introduces the themes of violent and natural death and the importance of good friends.

White solved his problem brilliantly, but to my mind he left himself with a new problem: what to do about Fern. Given the story's beginning, the reader has high hopes for Fern. But the story moves away from her. After finding Wilbur a home at her uncle's nearby barn, Fern takes no other important actions.

There also seems to be something awkward about first focusing on Fern, who turns out to be a minor character, and then taking up with Wilbur, who turns out to be so passive, and not introducing Charlotte until the end of chapter 4. At that point, Charlotte enters in firm command, the active heroine who takes charge of everything, including the wandering narrative.

According to Neumeyer, White later wrote that Fern was "built-in" to the story. Some critics say that her growth—in a few summer months—from an eight-year-old who communed with animals to a preadolescent who loses interest in Wilbur and goes off with a boy is part of the theme of life's passages. Perhaps. In any case, White's storytelling is so strong that readers hardly notice Fern's absence—and many who do aren't concerned by it. A story with an imperfect structure can still be wonderful.

What can you learn from all this? Clearly, it pays to work on your story's beginning. There are many points at which you can enter your story: with any character, anywhere, at the first chronological event or anytime thereafter, filling in background fully or in brief summary later. You can even begin at the climax, letting the beginning and end of the climactic event frame the rest of the story, all told in flashback.

Consider your entry point carefully, but don't let difficulty resolving the problem bog you down. You may not get the first pages right until after you've written an entire first draft, when you know for sure where you're going and you're confident of your theme and your voice. Be aware as you write, and especially as you revise, that everything is connected: any change you make anywhere may have faraway effects.

Exercise

Although it's often best to start with your main character at the moment his or her story begins, try sketching out a different beginning for your novel. Start earlier or later than you had planned, in another setting, perhaps with a different character—someone far away who sets the plot in motion.

A different beginning may give new color to your story, bring it closer to your vision for it, or give you a new vision of what it can be. A different beginning may mean a livelier start for your reader.

EIGHTEEN

What about Point of View?

> They both always opened a book eagerly and suspiciously looking first to see whether or not it was an "I" book. If it were they would put it aside, not reading it until there was absolutely nothing else.
>
> —Eleanor Estes, *Ginger Pye*

People—writers and many readers—feel strongly about point of view. Writers are also often mightily confused about it.

No two writing texts seem to give the same number of choices of point of view or to define them in the same way. One text describes three kinds of first person and six kinds of third person. Another lists a total of six, four of them in first person. Some subcategories have complex literary titles, such as "First Person Peripheral" (Wayne Ude in "Teaching Point of View") and "Multiple Selective Omniscience" (Norman Friedman in "Point of View in Fiction").

Do writing teachers make such a to-do about point of view only because it's complex and seems infinitely definable and subdefinable, thus available for endless analysis? Possibly. But the point of view from which your story is told *is* important. An inconsistent, unclear, or overcomplicated point of view makes readers uneasy. They ask, How does the narrator know that—she wasn't there? Is that the author or the character talking? How can the narrator tell what he's thinking?

In fact, there are just a few decisions to make. Most simply, the choice is between a first-person story (using "I") and third-person story (using "she" or "he").

Whether you use the first or third person, the other basic question for you is the one introduced into the national consciousness during the Watergate hearings: "What did the president know and when did he know it?" For "president" substitute both "narrator" and "reader." You must be cognizant of your narrator's *and* your reader's understanding of events at every point. Your choice of point of view is one way to control this.

Sometimes answering the question What does he or she know? is a simple matter; at other times it's quite complex. A good part of the power of *The Adventures of Huckleberry Finn* comes from Huck's clear-eyed but often innocent narration. Although he's a reliable reporter of facts, he doesn't always understand their meaning. Humor and poignancy thus are rooted in the reader's deeper comprehension of what's going on.

These two choices—first or third, and how much does the narrator know—seem straightforward, yet problems arise because each choice presents a sliding continuum of complexity and involvement in the plot. For instance, you might use several first-person narrators, each of whom knows a different aspect of the story.

When asked about point of view, I used to feel that the questioner was dutifully following a script and that I must respond dutifully with something profound and conclusive. I didn't. I simply said, Know that there are several stances from which a story can be told and that probably one will best suit the story you're telling. Once you've made a choice, the basic rule applies: Be clear and consistent.

I was forced to take a closer look at the problem when one group of writers in my workshop handed in chapters loaded with point-of-view problems. These enthusiastic writers wanted to include every great idea and every great effect they could think of. If a good line occurred to them, they flipped from one character's thoughts to another's so they could use it. They jumped in between the reader and the story to laugh at the fix a character was in. Their narrators told us things they couldn't possibly know. They abandoned their stories altogether to pile in undigested character sketches or historical research. In one story, the first paragraph took place inside a dog's mind, the next gave a boy's thoughts, the third looked on as dog and boy tumbled together at the far end of the yard.

These writers wrote well, but they were self-indulgent, ungoverned by a sense of obligation to their readers. I grappled for something useful, some bedrock principle, with which to rein in this undisciplined creativity. My mind flashed back to my first novel, where I'd had my own point-of-view problem.

I told that story in the first person, working smoothly until chapter 12, after my narrator had been kidnapped. I wanted to show his charming, quicksilver friend, a kid who didn't speak much English, figuring things out and alerting the boy's father to what had happened. I solved the problem easily—or so I thought—by switching to third person for a scene between father and friend.

My editor explained to me that throwing a third-person chapter into a first-person story so late would be disconcerting to readers, a jarring break in the narrative flow. I fought back long and hard, giving her all kinds of clever literary justifications for what I wanted to do. Finally she told me, in so many polite words, to grow up. That's not bad as a bedrock principle.

After backing down, I found that playing by the rule of consistency—staying in the first person with my kidnapped hero as he wondered what would happen—worked very well. Not only did the story progress more smoothly, but it was more suspenseful and interesting. As a bonus, after the rescue I could show father and friend together in a scene written from my hero's point of view, telling him about their comical meeting.

Restraint may not be comfortable at first, but if you accept a discipline and work within it your story is more likely to feel of a single piece. Your readers are more likely to stay submerged in your make-believe.

Choosing a point of view is likely to be intuitive. If one point of view seems integral to your story, that's what you'll use. Still, there may be trouble ahead, so it's worth being alert and knowing something about the choices.

A first-person narrator is most often the protagonist telling his or her own story. This can give readers a valuable sense of closeness to the central character. But a first-person narrative can also lapse into a tedious one-note, as when the first person is used to show off the narrator's wise-cracking ability or deliver endless, whiny complaints.

The use of a first-person narrative may force a narrow view, for you'll be limited to scenes where that person is present. You can have someone else tell the narrator what happened somewhere else, but that device wears thin.

In *Roll of Thunder, Hear My Cry,* the first-person narrator functions quite believably, from time to time, as a third-person reporter of events at which she is not actively present. The family lives in a home built for eavesdropping, with several enveloping porches and many connecting doors. The parents often tell the children to go away, and the children, who desperately need to learn what's going on, listen in. Thus the child narrator can believably report at length on wholly adult scenes.

If you use a third-person narrator, you have more choices. You may still describe the action from the limited point of view of a single character—not much more objective than first-person reporting—or you may give several perspectives on what's happening by following or going inside the minds of a number of characters. Is the narrator a cool, impersonal reporter who merely transmits information? Or someone who constantly comments, all hot and bothered by the goings-on?

Some writers use a narrator who can take readers into the mind of any character, to any scene at any time or place. A word of warning: the omniscient narrator may sound temptingly free, but the role is tricky to handle and hard to sustain realistically and effectively. Using an omniscient (unlimited *knowledge*) narrator does not make you omnipotent (unlimited *power*). You still have no right to flit here and there, dipping in and out of people's minds for immediate effect without considering the total story.

Gary Paulsen's *Hatchet*, a boy's survival story, is close to being a single-character story, yet it benefits from a third-person narrator. Paulsen allows the reader to watch Brian's efforts to find food and stay safe almost as if this were an impersonal report, yet he easily moves inside Brian's head for thoughts and dreams.

To tell your story effectively, to make your story whole, you must follow the rules of unity. You must work out your own consistent limits. How many characters will you follow? How much of their thoughts will you convey? Will you step back from time to time and speak as a more distant commentator? The story is your plaything only to a limited extent. You must make sure that your readers feel they are on solid, not shifting, ground.

In *Stone Fox*, John Gardiner does at times shift the point of view, and awkwardly. For most of the story the third-person narrative sticks closely to little Willy's perceptions, thoughts, and actions. Then suddenly readers are thrown into the minds of some townspeople to hear their conversation when little Willy does not. Briefly, they're alone with Stone Fox.

During the climactic race, this skittering about becomes almost frantic. Who's looking at whom? Who's thinking? Who's calling to whom?

> But little Willy still had a good lead. In fact, it was not until the last two miles of the race that Stone Fox got his first glimpse of little Willy since the race had begun.
>
> The five Samoyeds looked magnificent as they moved effortlessly across the snow. Stone Fox was gaining, and he was gaining fast. And little Willy wasn't aware of it.
>
> Look back, little Willy! Look back!

Because the story's momentum is so great by this time, readers may not slow down enough to be confused. Couldn't all the important information, including the beauty of the dogs, have been conveyed as well, or even more dramatically, while continuing to tell the story from little Willy's point of view?

Some author are adept at using several points of view clearly, and the narration strengthens their stories. Robert Cormier's *I Am the Cheese* mixes three kinds of narration, both first- and third-person, and could not be told to such riveting effect any other way. Cormier controls his device so that readers are at ease with *how* the story is told even while confused, as they're meant to be, about *what* is being told and how much the various narrators know.

Consistency and clarity of point of view allow readers to give themselves over to a novel without reserving part of their minds for checking up on the author. If, as in Cormier's book, there's something unusual in your point of view, show this early, clearly, and often so that your readers will accept it as the convention of your novel.

Beginning writers often want to know whether it's better to use the first or third person. In deciding, think of your reader's involvement with the story. Will an urgent, concerned "I" make him or her care more? Or might a strong, highly self-conscious "I" stand between the reader and what's happening? Does the scale of your novel perhaps require the greater freedom and range of a third-person narrative? The hazard that the narrative's point of view will become a barrier rather than a bridge between reader and story is greater in the first person. A good rule is: when in doubt, use the third person.

One reason critics have had such trouble with definitions of points of view may be that each well-written novel is a unique creation and each narrator stands in unique relation to events. Whether in a third-person story the narrator can enter the minds of one or all of the characters is a function of that individual story, not of an abstract rule. Since the limitations on what any narrator knows and tells come from both characters and circumstances, not from a literary chart, the possibilities for each book are different, and its author must make the rules.

Exercise

If you're in doubt about which point of view will be most effective, writing two-page summaries or a sample scene several ways may help. Take a brief two-person scene in your story and write it five times: once in the omniscient third person, once in the third person from the point of view of each character, then twice more, letting each character narrate.

Writing and rereading these summaries should give you a good sense of which point of view best suits your vision of the novel. You also may learn more about the scene and the meaning it has for each participant. Whatever point of view you end up using, you'll probably include in your story some insight gleaned from this exercise.

NINETEEN

How Do I Handle Dialogue?

"[A]nd what is the use of a book," thought Alice, "without pictures or conversations?"

—Lewis Carroll, *Alice's Adventures in Wonderland*

As usual, Alice is quite right—and the story of her adventures comes through with plenty of lively dialogue and intriguing pictures.

Dialogue can offer a pleasure akin to illustrations. Visually, a page full of dialogue comes as a relief after a thick body of narrative or descriptive text. Dialogue gives readers a refreshing change in voice. Since dialogue is part of a scene, it allows readers to experience the characters firsthand, without the narrator intervening. It has the added impact of showing, not telling.

Your characters' conversations can propel the plot, reveal personalities and motivations, foreshadow events, and entertain. Dialogue is richest when it does several things at once: when a person speaks in a characteristic voice, gives readers vital information, *and* makes them laugh out loud.

Edith Wharton is quoted in Dorothea Brande's *Becoming a Writer* as saying that dialogue "should be reserved for the culminating moments, and regarded as the spray into which the great wave of narrative breaks in curving toward the watcher on the shore." A scene in Laura Ingalls Wilder's *Little House on the Prairie* illustrates how a speech can top off the narrative to climactic effect. The Ingalls family has been traveling in its horse-drawn wagon for days and sets out again one morning on what seems to readers, and surely to Laura and Mary, to be a day like all the ones before:

When the sun rose, they were driving on across the prairie. There was no road now. Pet and Patty waded through the grasses, and the wagon left behind it only the tracks of its wheels.

Before noon, Pa said, "Whoa!" The wagon stopped.

"Here we are, Caroline!" he said. "Right here we build our new house."

Laura and Mary scrambled over the feed-box and dropped to the ground in a hurry. All around them there was nothing but grassy prairie spreading to the edge of the sky.

Much is accomplished here as Pa relates his family to the setting, speaking to his wife, not to his children, in his role as family leader. The rest of the plot springs from this simple, decisive speech.

How can you make dialogue lively and interesting? For starters, don't use it where it's not needed. As Wharton suggests, much of a story can be told or shown effectively through narrative. "I need some toothpaste. Let's go to the drugstore" is pure, boring traffic management. You'd be better off simply telling your readers what the plans are.

Here's a scene from A. A. Milne's *Winnie-the-Pooh* wherein making plans—in this case, to rid the forest of newcomers Kanga and Roo—results in wonderful dialogue:

"The best way," said Rabbit, "would be this. The best way would be to steal Baby Roo and hide him, and then when Kanga says, 'Where's Baby Roo?' we say *Aha!*"

"*Aha!*" said Pooh, practicing. "*Aha! Aha!* . . . Of course," he went on, "we could say 'Aha!' even if we hadn't stolen Baby Roo."

"Pooh," said Rabbit kindly, "You haven't any brain."

"I know," said Pooh humbly.

"We say 'Aha!' so that Kanga knows that *we* know where Baby Roo is. 'Aha!' means 'We'll tell you where Baby Roo is, if you promise to go away from the Forest and never come back.' Now don't talk while I think."

The scene is funny, it shows readers about the characters, and it hints at a lively confrontation to come.

Two-character dialogue involves just one relationship. A three-person scene, with three relationships, is often more interesting. With three characters in the scene, readers don't know who will speak next or to whom. Think of the three sides of a triangle as opposed to the single back-and-forth line between just two speakers. Think of a square, complete with corner-to-corner diagonals: four characters present in a scene means six relationships in play— which could be fun or could become confusing.

How can you make your characters' speeches lifelike? In some novels the voices used in dialogue seem to be the same as the narrative voice, with no change in vocabulary, diction, or energy— in other words, they're not the way real people talk.

But writing the way real people talk isn't exactly the answer, either. A great deal of what people say is said at too great length or in snippets or is repeated. There's no need to say much of what's said. If you're feeling brave, run a tape recorder during a family supper and then transcribe the conversation. Probably no family could surmount that challenge. The tedious job of transcription will probably end any desire you have to write "realistic" dialogue.

You do want the *feeling* of actual speech, however. The trick is to distill natural talk so that it *seems* real yet keeps the story moving and interesting. Reading novels with particular attention to the dialogue can help you. As you write, keep in mind the words each character uses as well as the different voices he or she may use when talking with different people. Finally, listen hard, particularly to children. Invent, write, and then cut and shape what you've written. Read your dialogue aloud, perhaps into a tape recorder so you can replay it. Let your ears pick up what your eyes may miss. Then rewrite again.

Full-scale adoption of unusual language is tricky. Using slang or dialect to liven things up may be tempting, and it may even suit your story in spots, but too much may make readers so conscious of the telling that they won't be able to enjoy the story itself. Dialect is hard to sustain, and your lapses will be disturbing to alert readers. Authors who use dialect seem prone to using dialect clichés instead of thinking out the words and sounds for themselves. They often use quaint, cute language that can be irritating or numbing to read. It's probably best to simply indicate here and there that a character speaks in a particular way—and then get on with the story.

Writers I've known seem to have more trouble with punctuating speech than with any other aspect of grammar. If you're in doubt, your best guide would be the way dialogue is punctuated in published stories.

Take a look at the Pooh books as a model for writing dialogue that's interesting and lively, as well as for a treat. Milne, a playwright, knew how to make his wee plots advance through his characters' nattering on. After setting up a scene so readers know who's present, Milne often doesn't tell us who speaks each line—he doesn't have to, for we recognize their familiar voices. You could spend a happy morning reading Pooh.

Exercise

Write a two-sentence speech for a character to give at a crucial point in your story. Make the speech do several things—for example, give new information about the setting, deepen the reader's understanding of a character's motivation, move the plot, or heighten a mystery. Then write a second speech by the same character at the same place in the story but emphasize other qualities.

This exercise should help you sense what a flexible tool dialogue can be. If you're still in doubt that a speech can do so much, pick up a good novel and read some dialogue at random.

TWENTY

The Words Themselves

We are very graceful that you came.

—A fourth-grader, thanking me for teaching his class

The questions people ask most often about writing for children are about the writing itself. Just as many adults alter their voices when speaking to children, many think they must alter their voices when writing for children. The effect is the same: contrived.

As any good librarian will tell you, the fit between a child and a book depends on the child, the moment, and the mood. A child who lies in a hammock most of a summer afternoon absorbed in *Jane Eyre* may be found in bed that evening absorbed in an Archie comic.

A novel for new readers should not be intimidating. Don't make the paragraphs and chapters so long, so dense, that you scare off your readers. Beyond that, what's the proper length and texture? A hour in the library should give you a sense of the range. Unless you're writing for a line of books with exact specifications, it's best to make a story just as long as it takes you to tell it well. If a chapter feels too long to you, it will probably feel too long to your readers. Trust your instincts.

The saddest question I hear is about limiting vocabulary to make it age-appropriate. In our fine-tuning culture, there *are* books that list vocabulary by grade, even grade-month. There are probably editors who require authors to write according to such lists. I've never met one. No editor has asked me to change a word because it's too difficult. The greater danger is in writing too young. It's better to write somewhat over readers' heads than to talk down to them. Here, again, your instinct is a good guide.

The recommended ages for William Steig's *Dominic* are eight to twelve—roughly third through seventh grades, a wide range. Here are the opening paragraphs:

> Dominic was a lively one, always up to something. One day, more restless than usual, he decided there wasn't enough going on in his own neighborhood to satisfy his need for adventure. He just had to get away.
>
> He owned an assortment of hats which he liked to wear, not for warmth or for shade or to shield him from rain, but for their various effects—rakish, dashing, solemn, or martial. He packed them together with his precious piccolo and a few other things, in a large bandanna which he tied to the end of a stick so it could be carried easily over a shoulder.

Is Steig's vocabulary inappropriate for his intended readers? I looked up thirteen long or unusual words from these paragraphs in one of the vocabulary guides. Eight words weren't even listed.

How tedious reading would be if all authors relied on prescribed vocabulary lists! One reason Steig's stories are so dear to children, and to adults, is because he *does* throw out words like "martial" and "rakish" that many readers may not know. When the context is as rich and interesting as *Dominic,* when the voice is as confident and promising as this one, readers will sail along on the story, learning a few new words (or not), looking them up (or not), making out the meaning from the context (or not) as they go along. It doesn't matter much, does it? What's a piccolo? If it's important to the story, readers will learn.

It's true that a child reader may give up on a book that contains many long and unfamiliar words jammed together in long, unrelieved paragraphs. But who would write that way for children? On the other hand, if a long or complex passage feels right, and unchangeable, perhaps you should try it. One never is absolutely sure how children will react. There is, for instance, this story:

To encourage kids to use paragraphs in their writing, I used to hold up *Absalom, Absalom!*, open to a dense, unparagraphed two-page spread. Next to it I held a spread from almost any other novel, with short paragraphs, plenty of dialogue, and lots of inviting white space.

"Which would you rather read?"

The unanimous favorite was always the well-paragraphed work.

"I would too," I'd answer pointedly. "Please use paragraphs in the stories you give me."

Then one class flocked behind its leader to vote unanimously for the Faulkner. Incredulous, I asked why. Enthusiastically, thrilled to be proving me wrong, they shouted out the obvious advantage: "You get more!"

Beyond comments focused on child readers in particular, some useful things can be said about writing in general. It's important to write well—not brilliantly, but well. A momentary confusion, even one wrong word, could jar a reader out of deep involvement with your story. Careless writing also signals a publisher that your manuscript, however rich and inventive its story, will need a daunting (expensive) amount of editorial work to make it a book.

So how can you be sure that your novel is well written? Most advice about writing is common sense. Some useful goals are clarity, consistency, effective word placement, and selection. It's also helpful to think of grammar and punctuation not as a teacher's or editor's set of rules and restrictions but as traffic signals that can help you to guide your readers smoothly through your story.

Clarity

Your basic responsibility is to tell your story as clearly as possible. Help yourself do this by putting the manuscript aside for a while before rereading it. Sneak up on it and require the story *as written* to make you understand.

Giving your story several careful rereadings is only the first step. Regarding clarity, you're not to be fully trusted—you know your story too well. Show it to others and pay close attention to how they respond. Ask your readers to mark any place where they're even briefly confused.

Consistency

As with clarity, consistency helps the reader stay concentrated on the story. Be sure that motivations are consistent with character and that the one-way street mentioned in chapter 1 doesn't become a two-way street in chapter 5. Consistency is especially important in fantasy stories, where you're making up the rules. If you yield to the temptation to be indiscriminately "creative," you may leave your readers stranded in a confusing morass.

Since the story is consistent in your own mind, it's hard for *you* to catch inconsistencies on paper. Ask a careful reader to be alert for inconsistencies. Reading your story aloud to yourself can also help.

Placement

By "placement" I mean what comes when: what comes first and, especially, what comes last. Awkward, dull, or confusing writing often can be helped by changing the placement of words or phrases within a sentence or sentences within a paragraph. Closely related words usually belong together. Events are best presented in the order in which they happen. But placement is also a more subtle, and supple, narrative tool.

Every word, every phrase is not created equal. A long stretch of unweighted information may confuse and bore readers, who won't know what to keep in mind as they read on. Readers need your guidance as they move through your story.

In general, keep your prose working forward. Put setting-up material at the beginning of a sentence, squirrel away necessary but bland information in the middle, and put the exciting news, the words that urge the reader onward, in the strongest position, which is at the end. That highly promising sentence from Robert Louis Stevenson's *Treasure Island* about the closed sea-chest (see page 28) is the last in a paragraph of mostly interchangeable sentences that describe a pirate's clothing and habits. The last word in that last sentence is "open." Readers note the hint and wait to see what's inside.

Consider these two sentences:

At last Dick and Jane saw the open field bathed in sunlight beyond the thick stand of giant trees.

At last, beyond the thick stand of giant trees, Dick and Jane saw the open field, bathed in sunlight.

Which one works better? I prefer the second. It mirrors the children's search for a way out of the woods and leaves readers ready to move with them into the golden field.

Placement is neither a cure-all nor an end in itself. There's no need to check it in every sentence. Not every sentence must be a transition to the next. Sometimes forward momentum is better served by having the strongest words lead off. Writing all sentences according to a formula makes for dreary prose. It's more effective to vary sentences in placement, momentum, and length. But as you edit your work for clarity and impact, if you're trying to figure out why a passage is sluggish or a sentence doesn't seem to work, then examining the order of its parts may take you to the heart of the problem.

It *is* a good idea to check what you've put at the end of each section or chapter of your novel and at the start of the next. These transitions should be clear and vivid, nailing down the effect of one scene and raising expectations for what's to come.

Plain and Fancy Writing

Never underestimate the power of the plain truth. Simple, direct accounts are always welcome.

Fancy writing, on the other hand, can lead an author astray. If an effect of which you're particularly fond is there for its own sake rather than because it helps the story, then it may distract readers. The cure, suggested by Sir Arthur Quiller-Couch in *The Art of Writing,* is simple, if drastic: "Murder your darlings."

A friend who read my manuscripts often singled out for praise a word here and a phrase there. I was pleased until I noticed that these were always words and phrases that called attention to themselves. I learned to take a hard look at whatever my friend admired and consider it a candidate for murder.

Rich, colorful, highly evocative writing can bring added pleasure to readers. If you can write beautifully *and* clearly *and* not sidetrack readers, then by all means do so. But first, as the doctors say, do no harm.

Strong and Weak Words

Nouns and verbs—subject and action—usually have more potency than adjectives and adverbs. Particularly when these descriptive words are strung together as if to strengthen an effect, they often do the opposite, diluting the reader's interest.

Sentences that lack a subject or a verb create a different problem. They're used, I think, to enliven prose. To punch it up. But often they're overused or badly used. Add a stop and start quality. Highly annoying.

Beginning an occasional sentence with a conjunction—"and," "but," and "or"—can be effective. But it's usually best to complete the thought in a single sentence. Bland words like "it" and "this," while sometimes useful, provide little information or color. Passive voice ("A huge meal was eaten by Sally") is not as interesting or engaging as active voice ("Sally ate a huge meal"). Sometimes all it takes is a quick look through your manuscript to find places where you can substitute richer, more interesting words.

Clichés

Just as the author's mind goes on automatic pilot for a nanosecond as he or she types "dead as a doornail," so the reader's mind will turn off as he or she reads that cliché. The words, and thus the story, are briefly abandoned of meaning. Better to use "dead as a goldfish that wasn't fed for a week" or "dead as the fifteenth rerun of 'Happy Days,'" choosing a simile that fits the setting or a quality in your character and one that young readers are more likely to understand.

No writer always has the perfect words handy. As you go, you may be aware of using a cliché or other words that aren't as good as you want them to be. Some writers edit and change as they go, but I like to keep going, to sustain my momentum, so I type "ICK" or "AWK" after offending words before going on. These remind me to come back and work a little harder.

Fantasy seems to attract clichéd, or trite, prose, as if the writers have simply plugged into an entire, too-familiar scheme of incidents, language, even the naming of characters and places. Borrowed heightened language won't do the job, nor will oddly spelled names with too few vowels or sudden random bits of magic. For a fantasy story to be sustained and involving, the language must be clear and original, evoking the special world the author creates. Fantasy voices with perfect pitch, to my ear, are heard in Mary Norton's *The Borrowers*, Daniel Pinkwater's *Blue Moose*, Virginia Hamilton's *The House of Dies Drear*, Diana Wynne Jones's *Dogsbody*, William Steig's *Dominic*, Robin McKinley's *Beauty*, Ruth Stiles Gannett's *My Father's Dragon*, Joan Aiken's *Nightbirds on Nantucket*, and Lewis Carroll's *Alice's Adventures in Wonderland*.

Repetition

Repetition can strengthen a story, as when evocative words, phrases, and even scenes are used again and again to reinforce meaning and provide a sense of continuity. Bible stories, mythology, and fairy tales all repeat words and event patterns to strong effect. In the novels I've discussed, think of Charlotte weaving a web-word again and again. Think of the Tin Woodsman's recurring joint troubles. Think of the honey Pooh consumes. Think of the patterns of trust and loyalty, distrust and disloyalty, that Jim Hawkins must learn and unlearn about his fellow sailors. These repetitions enhance our pleasure and our understanding, as the authors intended.

Repetition can also be a nagging bore. Words or incidents that closely mimic a predecessor without meaningful change or useful reinforcement or cumulative humor may make your readers long for graceful synonyms or more creative energy on your part. That said, don't fall into the trap of grabbing at some word, almost any word, to avoid repetition. Much better the exact word, repeated, than a pale approximation used for variety's sake. If repetition enhances your story, then don't be afraid to use it.

Don't engage in thesaurus-contortion to avoid repeating the word "said." "Said" quickly and economically does what you need—attaches a speaker to a speech. When you want to characterize, use the words of the speech or a gesture by the speaker.

With repetition, as with much else in writing, the final test is your own response as you reread and rewrite.

Exercises

Go to a sentence or a paragraph in your story that has been bothering you, one that seems awkward or bland or unclear. See if careful attention to word placement will improve it.

Take a single page of your story at random and carefully study the writing. Look for sentences that are unclear, for the most effective placement of words and phrases within sentences and paragraphs, for repetitions that jar, for clichés or clichéd writing, for dialogue that is just talk. Does the writing point the reader forward? Is there florid language you should eliminate? Can you cut the page by 25 percent and keep the meaning clear?

Now go back and be sure you haven't edited the life out of the page. Did you find any recurring problems that you should keep in mind as you edit the whole novel?

PART SIX

Finally

TWENTY-ONE

Revising and Editing

> In my experience of writing, you generally start out with some overall idea that you can see fairly clearly, as if you were standing on a dock and looking at a ship on the ocean. At first you can see the entire ship, but then as you begin work you're in the boiler room and you can't see the ship anymore. All you can see are the pipes and the grease and the fittings of the boiler room, and you have to *assume* the ship's exterior. What you really want in an editor is someone who's still on the dock, who can say, Hi, I'm looking at your ship, and it's missing a bow, the front mast is crooked, and it looks to me as if your propellers are going to have to be fixed.
>
> —Michael Crichton, *The Paris Review* (Fall 1994)

> Revising is part of writing. Few writers are so expert that they can produce what they are after on the first try. . . . Remember, it is no sign of weakness or defeat that your manuscript ends up in need of major surgery. This is a common occurrence in all writing, and among the best writers.
>
> —William Strunk Jr. and E. B. White, *The Elements of Style*

One summer afternoon I took an armful of promising novels home from the library. I opened one, and before I'd read two pages I shut it. I went to the kitchen to make a big mug of coffee. The hint of vibrant complexity to come, the rumble of characters clashing, and the wit let me know this was a book to sink into and enjoy.

When revising, you want to make sure that your story is told as well as possible so that your reader will be satisfied. Satisfaction may seem to be a vague and tepid goal but, defined in different ways, this is what a reader wants. Satisfaction seems to be rooted in an author's passionate involvement with the story and sure sense of its whole, transmitted with careful attention to the reader's needs. Even an unhappy ending can be satisfying if it feels right and seems inevitable or if the central character has changed in the course of the story so that he or she will be able to deal more effectively with the hazards of life.

Making your story satisfying for readers takes your thoughtful rereading and, almost inevitably, revision. Before you give your story to anyone else to read, do as much as you can yourself to make it the story you want it to be. What counts is not the glorious novel you had in your mind but what's on the page. If you imagined your central character to be wonderfully charming, but she thinks nothing charming, says nothing charming, does nothing charming on paper, then she won't charm your reader.

You'll need to gain some distance from your story so that you can see it *as you wrote it*. Cleanse your mental palate with a week or more away from the story and then read it as if for the first time. Respond to the story as directly as you can before you analyze whether or how it's working. If you find a problem, make a brief note in the margin and keep reading. You want a full sense of the flowing story.

Once you begin to revise, be wary of using quick and easy, "logical" solutions for problems. Think about them for a while and then try to solve them from *within* the story, rather than by tacking on a quick fix. Often there's already an aspect of a character or situation that will help you do exactly what's needed. Why *did* Joe wait till well into the autumn to leave Cincinnati, as your plot requires him to do? You don't have to make the Ohio River suddenly flood in order to delay him. Let the answer come from digging deeper into your understanding of all that motivates Joe. Of course! His beloved Reds won the pennant that year, and he wanted to hang around until the World Series was over.

Likewise, think carefully before you solve a problem by simply eliminating it. Sometimes a speech or a scene will seem wrong because it doesn't belong in the story; but if the problem is true to your characters and your plot, then dealing with it may be important to the story. Ask yourself how your characters would handle the problem: they may, in effect, suggest a solution to you. The rapid change in Fern's behavior in *Charlotte's Web* might seem more believable if she or the animals reacted to her growing distance from the barnyard. White does try a version of this, having a doctor tell Fern's mother, "It's amazing how children change from year to year."

It's never too late to try directing a summary at a specific problem. Should this chapter go before or after that one? Does the story work better within the school year or during the summer? Writing a summary each way may help you assess the value of alternative solutions and work out useful changes. Go back to your first vision of the story or your theme as you identified it and use these as plumb lines against which to test possible solutions.

Your next step might be to read the whole novel aloud to a trusted and tolerant friend, perhaps on a long car trip. Watch your listener as you read what you hope is a coherent, involving story. Try to sense when he or she is impatient or understands too little or too much. Facial expressions and body language may show that a sequence, exposition, or emphasis must be changed, or that a scene badly needs cutting. Note every ad lib you throw in to help your listener understand and enjoy the story. Mark the paragraphs and half sentences you leave out because they now seem irrelevant or dull. Listen for writing that calls attention to itself and away from the story. You'll be painfully aware of flaws and pleasantly surprised—or perhaps devastated—when an ordinary passage turns out to be laugh-out-loud funny.

It's important to try out your story on people who read it to themselves. When you're ready to give the manuscript to someone to read, make it inviting, easy to read, and easy to write comments on. Type it neatly or print it out on one side of the paper using double-spacing and wide margins. Number the pages. Proofread it carefully. A reader's valuable attention shouldn't be wasted on typographical errors.

An experienced writer helped me greatly with one of my manuscripts. He alerted me to unclear action and unbelievable motivation. He told me when his expectations for a scene were not met. He told me when good material was in the wrong place, where it was less useful or satisfying. He told me where the story felt repetitive or confused as to direction and when he wished to enjoy a scene a little longer. That's the kind of help every writer longs for.

If you give your story to someone who is inexperienced at reading manuscripts, make sure they know that you're asking not for praise but for explicit responses, both positive and negative. (Negative responses may hurt initially, but they can prove more valuable.) The job of manuscript readers is to point out problems, ask questions, note when they're disappointed or pleased, and generally let you know how a reader experiences your story.

Encourage your readers to mark up your manuscript as they go along rather than waiting to summarize their responses at the end. You want to know exactly where they're bored, confused, or amused, exactly where they don't believe that a character would do what he or she has done. Marginal notes like "You already told me that" or "Am I supposed to know who she is?" or "I thought you said she lived *up* the hill" are helpful. Comments such as "Getting exciting!" or "He's impossible!" let you know how a reader responds at various points.

What you don't want from these readers are solutions—those must come from you. When a reader tries to fix your story for you, to solve a problem quickly and cleverly, remember that you know your story best. Find out, if you can, why the reader has a problem and then deal with it in your own way. An early reader of this book thought I should cut out the Horatio Alger epigraph in the interlude "Didacticism versus Vicarious Experience": "It's so boring!" she wrote. Well, that was part of my point. Instead of cutting it, I added a warning.

When you give someone your manuscript, tell them that no question or comment is too dumb to jot down. Likewise, no question is so dumb that *you* can ignore it. Listen to everything anyone says about your manuscript. Every comment comes from the reader's experience with your written words. If a reader wasn't paying attention, ask yourself *why* his or her mind might have wandered. Each reader brings his or her own personality and experiences to a story, and these may clash with your intent and your judgment of what's important. Although you may eventually decide to disregard a comment, do, if only for a moment, consider why it was made.

I briefly told a friend about a story I was working on and she expressed concern because my hero had no child friends: "Friends are everything at that age." She was right about that—but wrong about my hero. James had no friends for good reasons. Still, it was useful to know that I ought to explain why early on.

While someone is talking to you about your manuscript, try to keep your ears and eyes open and your mouth shut, except when you need to clarify a response for yourself or test an idea for revision. If you have the urge to explain things or convince a reader of something, do it when you're alone again with your manuscript—by rewriting that part of your story.

As you revise, enriching your story with all you have learned by writing it, remember that any change you make may affect or distort a distant scene. When you alter something, first read its immediate context and then consider its impact on the rest of the story. The better you can think through all the ramifications of a change, the more likely you'll be able to integrate it successfully.

Revision is hard work and may be hard on the ego. It's not fun to take out words you worked hard to put in. For each revision I keep a separate "outtake" file of material that's halfway to oblivion. Any words that probably should be cut but I hate to give up go in that file. Later, I review the outtakes and, just occasionally, return some gem to my manuscript.

A manuscript often gets worse before it gets better. There's a rhythm in writing that involves first indulging your imagination as you create lovely new touches, even scenes, then editing the work to tighten and clarify, then loosening the restraints again. This alternation can go on for most of the revision process. Often, the draft you print out after a careful editing will seem tighter and smoother but somewhat flat. The next draft—as you play with your story again, adding fresh material to the cleaner narrative line—should be much better.

Don't be surprised that writing and revising take much longer than you expected. New writers often wonder, rather irritably, how long it's supposed to take to write a book. The question is natural but can be destructive. The answer is: It takes as long as it takes.

People who ask this may be thinking, "A children's novel should be easy to write. I'll just knock one off," then are surprised at how hard it is to write a publishable manuscript. Maybe they're aware of Ann M. Martin, who published (with help) several books a month in her Baby-Sitters Club series and its spinoffs, or Phyllis Reynolds Naylor, who writes several accomplished and widely read novels each year. Those authors are exceptional.

When your confidence flags, think instead about Maurice Sendak, who took two years to write (not illustrate) *Where the Wild Things Are*. Sendak says that he "spent five years in solitary confinement writing *Outside Over There*, which has 351 words" (*New York Times Magazine*, Oct. 12, 1980). Obviously he didn't sit at his desk every hour of every day for two years or five trying to decide what word should come next. The point is that it took him that long to understand fully what his story was and to make it what he wanted it to be.

The important thing is to work until you get it right. Doing a good job of writing usually means doing a good job of *re*writing, and then rewriting again. It doesn't matter whether you're fast or slow. Comparing yourself to anyone else doesn't make sense.

There may come a time, however, when you've been working on a novel for years and the life has gone out of your desire to tell that particular story. Perhaps you've learned all you can from working on it. There's a reason a story comes to you at a given time in your life. Maybe that time has passed. If you find yourself in this situation, put the work aside and give yourself the energizing boost of a fresh start on new material. Maybe you'll get back to the first novel someday; maybe the deep feeling that inspired it will return. Maybe not.

Exercises

Write a summary stressing the most important thing that happens in each chapter or section of your novel. Is the material adequately weighted so its importance will be clear to the reader? This exercise is useful late in your work, giving you a fresh tack for re-entering your narrative.

Make a list of questions you'd like to ask a thoughtful reader about your draft novel. Your reader may be a child, an adult friend, or an editor, and you may have different questions for each.

Now ask the questions of yourself first. The better you know your manuscript and your own convictions and doubts about it, the better use you'll be able to make of readers' comments.

Add to your list any useful questions based on what previous readers have told you.

TWENTY-TWO

A Process for Writing Children's Novels

Here are brief descriptions of work that might be useful as you prepare, draft, and revise your children's novel. These suggestions are in no specific order except for the first and last. This process works for me, though I certainly don't do everything on this list for each novel I write.

- Record and *save the spark* that makes you want to write this story. What about it first appealed to you? What matters most?
- *Muck around* in the material, free-associate. Anywhere, anytime, jot down anything you think of that belongs in the novel.
- Make a *plan for the specifics* of the book: age of readers, probable length, tone you'll use, divisions. Revise the plan as often as necessary, sharpening your sense of the book.
- *Research* any areas—local history, slug trails, white-collar crime—that you'll cover in your novel, even if you know them well. Facts and pictures will feed your subconscious. Doing research early will keep you from locking errors into your plot. Take careful notes.
- Make lists with information about your *crucial characters:* their looks, personality, habits. Include plenty of incidental information.

- List your *settings,* the settings within settings, and their characteristics using the five senses (sight, sound, smell, taste, and touch) and your curiosity as guides. Explore the settings fully: by moonlight, in winter, when the door is locked.
- *Remember your audience:* think about children, watch children, talk with children, ask them what they think.
- Draft a *rough plot* in any form that's useful to you—brief summary, long summary, outline, chapter sketches. Do another.
- Draw *maps and diagrams* of the places your characters go. As you do, your mind may flash to possible scenes and incidents. Take notes or sketch out those incidents right away.
- Make a *timeline* of the events in your story. Decide in which season you'll set your earliest scene and thus when subsequent events will fall. Is the weather you'll need for a scene appropriate to the time of year? Does the story fall comfortably within the school year? Do your characters age?
- If you feel the need to be orderly, you can *arrange everything* you've done so far into master lists and prose sketches of characters, settings, and incidents. Use the sketches to try out different voices.
- Whenever you have an impulse to write a scene or incident, no matter where it falls in the novel, give in and *write* it. But keep on with this preparatory work.
- You've been making important decisions, perhaps without being aware of them. Take time to *think things through.* Why is the central character a boy? or a girl? How old is that character? Are you telling the story in the first or third person? Why? When is the story set? What is the family structure? Is there a pet? Most of these choices will seem inevitable to your story, but you may want to reconsider some.
- Start lists of possible *titles* for the book and for chapters.
- Write *summaries* telling the story to yourself from beginning

to end, again and again. Pay attention to the changes you make each time. This is another chance to try different voices.

- Keep notes about your *themes* as you go along in order to sharpen your understanding of what your story is about. Hold yourself back from any didactic intrusions.
- Lay out your material in detail. From your notes, lists, sketches, and summaries *allot to each chapter* the material you'll want to cover there.
- To better understand your story and for further stimulation, muse about the *cultural codes* inherent in your settings and how these affect your characters.
- If you're writing a *fantasy*, keep track of the special rules you're asking your readers to believe. It's best if there aren't too many, if they're important to the story, and if you introduce them early on and in a way that seems natural.
- If you haven't yet found a *voice* that seems right, try brief scenes or summaries in several voices.
- Review your *divisions* into chapters or sections. Consider the beginning and ending of each. Are the transitions smooth? Do they encourage the reader to continue reading?
- *Keep reading children's novels.*
- Begin to *write,* probably starting at the beginning. You may want to put all your preparatory material aside and write your story freely from all you already know about it. If you do use the chapter pages, outlines, maps, and lists, to guide and feed you as you go, feel free to digress from what you planned, to play around. You can always change things back.
- Don't torture yourself by *comparing your novel* to anyone else's. Don't compare your plot, your speed, your type face— nothing! Your work is your own.
- *If something isn't working* or you need to jolt your thinking off

an unproductive track, go back to appropriate chapters in this
book and try the exercises again. Study a sketch of your central character or a diagram of an important setting.

- *Keep writing.* Rewrite and polish each sentence as you go, or
  begin each working session by reviewing and editing what you
  wrote the session before, or just plow ahead—whatever suits
  you.
- Join a writers' group or trade manuscripts with *other writers,*
  both to get the benefits of their criticism and to sharpen your
  own editing skills.
- As you reach later chapters and the pace quickens, be certain
  your *central character* continues to be active and effective, not
  just present, as events swirl around him or her.
- Keep a list of *last sentences,* last paragraphs, or last scenes that
  might convey the sense of closure, of order and accomplish-
  ment, that helps bring a reader meaning and satisfaction. Successful endings are often at least partly unexpected, but the
  consequences must be believable, true to characters and plot.
- When you've completed a first draft, clear your mind by setting your manuscript aside. When you're ready, *reread* it and
  take notes about possible revisions.
- Check for *particular concerns:* Is the opening strong? Is the
  central character introduced so that readers will care about him
  or her? Is the point of view consistent? Does the energy seep
  away in the middle of your story? Do you give hints and not follow through on them? Are you being preachy? Do you know—
  and use—your theme? Add your own concerns to this list.
- Go over *each draft* several times, perhaps editing on screen first
  and then on hard copy. Try using a different color pen each
  time you read through the manuscript. Continue to read and
  revise as many times as it takes until you're satisfied.

- Try *reading your manuscript aloud*—to yourself or to someone else.
- When you have what you think is your last, best draft, one that's ready to be mailed to an agent or an editor, put it aside for two weeks. Then *read it again* to be sure.

TWENTY-THREE

And Now, Back to the Keyboard

> Every few weeks she would shut herself up in her room, put on her scribbling suit, and "fall into a vortex," as she expressed it, writing away at her novel with all her heart and soul, for till that was finished she could find no peace.
>
> —Louisa May Alcott, *Little Women*

Don't be alarmed to find yourself back where you started. You're in the only place a good story will come from, alone with your thoughts and your words, writing the story only you in all the world can tell.

I wish you good luck, hard work, and an interesting time along the way. Remember, there are children out there eager to sink into another good book.

Appendix
Getting Your Manuscript Published

"The trouble isn't making poems, the trouble's finding somebody that will listen to them."

... "I'll go to the chipmunk and say, 'If you'll give me six crickets I'll make a poem about you.' Really I'd do it for nothing, but they don't respect something if they get it for nothing. I'll say: 'For six crickets I'll do your portrait in verse.'"

—Randall Jarell, *The Bat-Poet*

So far, this book has focused on the novel you want to write, on helping you tell your story as well as possible. There's also the matter of getting it published. It's vital to do some homework and planning about publishers and agents before sending out your manuscript. Following links around the Internet will give you some sense of the commercial world of children's books. Here are some other suggestions.

Finding a Publisher

Which publishers might be right for your novel? Browsing at length and asking questions of knowledgeable people in libraries and bookstores, as well as reading reviews of children's books, will give you a sense of what's being published now and by whom.

Once you have a list of likely publishers, call those houses and ask for their catalogs and submission guidelines. You may be able to get a lot of this information from individual publishers' Web sites. Studying the catalogs will give you a clearer sense of the kind of books each house publishes.

When you call a publisher, be sure to confirm the mailing address for submissions (things change fast in publishing). Find out if they want an exclusive submission or if they don't mind being one of several publishers to whom you send your story simultaneously. If you can chat with whomever answers the phone, you may be able to find out which editor might be most interested in your story so that you can write directly to him or her.

The Children's Book Council is an organization of many children's book publishers. Its membership list, frequently updated, gives the names of some editors at each house along with addresses, phone numbers, and fax numbers; it also briefly describes what kinds of manuscripts the house is looking for, how many are published each year, and how to submit your manuscript. The list is available at <http://www.cbcbooks.org> or by contacting the CBC at 212-966-1990.

Literary Market Place is an annual reference volume that includes lists of publishers and agents as well as other resources. It tells which publishers deal in children's books, gives names, addresses, phone numbers, and fax numbers, and usually indicates how the various publishers prefer to be contacted as well as the preferred form for submissions. *LMP* is available at many libraries.

Publishers Weekly, the book industry magazine, is often available at libraries and at some newsstands and bookstores. *PW* carries articles about children's book publishing, children's bookstores and authors, and brief reviews of some about-to-be published titles. In February and July, *PW* runs thick preview issues on children's books for the coming season. Publishers' ads and brief descriptions of their lists may give you a sense of which houses are right for your novel. You can order these issues separately by calling 1-800-662-4445.

Some publishers are little more than printing houses, doing almost no editing and asking you to pay the cost of publishing your book. This leaves you with a large bill and the considerable problems of promotion and distribution. Avoid such businesses.

Agents

If you want help finding a publisher, you probably want an agent. You probably want one anyway, for three reasons.

1. Editors at publishing houses look on agents as first screeners. They

are likely to read a manuscript submitted by an agent sooner and with higher hopes than one you submit yourself.

2. If your manuscript is accepted for publication, you'll need an agent (or a lawyer who specializes in publishing law) to help you get a good deal and a fair contract. Contracts are growing ever more complex.

3. The editing/publication process can take several years, and with the publishing business in continual flux you may well need an agent as your advocate during this period. An editor may leave, a schedule may change, what you'd been told to expect may not happen. An agent in your corner can help you assess developments and fight for what you and your story need.

How do you find an agent? Many are listed in *Literary Market Place*. Browsing in the how-to-write sections of bookstores and libraries should turn up some leads. Writers' magazines often have articles on agents. You can also call the Association of Authors' Representatives at 212-252-3695 for information on how to order a list of members, a canon of ethics, and information on the role of an agent and how to find one. The Society of Children's Book Writers and Illustrators (see below) has a list, available to members, of some agents who handle children's books.

As with publishers, find out about individual requirements and procedures by calling a number of agents. Be extremely cautious about any agent who charges a fee to read or handle a manuscript (though some respectable agents do bill you for their phone, mailing, and copying costs). Reputable agents get paid from the writer's advances and royalties *after* a book is signed and published.

Submissions

When you contact an agent or a publisher you'll need to write either a query letter (asking if you may send your manuscript) or a submission letter (accompanying either the story outline and sample chapters or the entire manuscript). This letter is the first piece of your writing an agent or editor will read, so write it carefully.

Your letter should tell why, of all the letters and manuscripts received that day, the agent or editor should pay attention to yours. Give a brief summary of your story and describe its place in the market: age of the readers you're writing for, length, and what sets your story apart from similar ones. Explain why your novel will appeal to children. Tell a little about yourself, including any publishing history and your special qualifications for and interest in writing this particular story. Discuss illustrations only if you've done them yourself; otherwise, choosing the illustrator and overseeing any art are the publisher's prerogative. Although you will have checked to be sure this publisher doesn't require exclusive submission, if you are submitting your manuscript to several publishers at once it's best to mention this in your letter.

Manuscript submission guidelines are mostly common sense. It's in your best interest to send a clean, attractive packet that asks to be picked up and read. A neat typescript or good-quality computer printout is essential. Your manuscript should be double-spaced, on one side of the paper only, with generous margins and numbered pages. Include a table of contents, maps, genealogical tables—whatever is appropriate and will dress up your manuscript and attract a reader.

Keep a copy of the manuscript and all correspondence. You can copyright your unpublished work through the Library of Congress, though it's not necessary to register copyright for your work to be protected by U.S. copyright laws.

Enclose a large enough self-addressed stamped envelope (commonly known as a SASE) if you want your materials returned. If you want to be sure the package has arrived safely at the agent's or publisher's address, enclose a self-addressed stamped postcard. Package all of this carefully so that your submission arrives in good shape.

Be prepared for rejections. Remember that the lists of different houses vary; a manuscript declined by one may be just right for another. Keep a plan for where you want to send a manuscript next, so that you can turn it around quickly if it does come back.

Most rejections come without individualized comment, but if there *is* some inkling of why a publisher didn't want your story, if an editor takes the time to write, it means that something about your story interested him or her. Think seriously about the comments. *If* you think they have merit, try a revision. Then write or call that editor and ask if you may resubmit the manuscript.

It can be helpful to join a writers' organization. A large one with a newsletter will keep you up to date on writers' issues. A smaller local one will put you in touch with other writers. Either may help you feel more professional, as well as prepare you for the choices and problems you'll face in the commercial literary world.

The Society of Children's Book Writers and Illustrators has local branches and useful publications, including a newsletter. You don't have to be a published author to join. The address is 8271 Beverly Boulevard, Los Angeles, CA 90048. Their URL is <http://www.scbwi.org>; or call 323-782-1010.

JUDY K. MORRIS is the author of three children's novels—*The Crazies and Sam* (Viking, 1983), *The Kid Who Ran for Principal* (Lippincott, 1989), and *Nightwalkers* (HarperCollins, 1996)—as well as several nonfiction books for children. For nearly twenty years she was a weekly writing teacher in the Washington, D.C., public schools. She regularly teaches an eight-week workshop at the Writer's Center in Bethesda, Maryland, for adults writing novels for children.

Composed in 11/15 New Caledonia
with New Caledonia, Trade Gothic, and Veljovic display
by Celia Shapland
for the University of Illinois Press
Designed by Paula Newcomb
Manufactured by Thomson-Shore, Inc.

University of Illinois Press
1325 South Oak Street
Champaign, IL 61820-6903
www.press.uillinois.edu